The Undying Lamp of Zen

ALSO BY THOMAS CLEARY

Awakening to the Tao
The Book of Balance and Harmony
The Inner Teachings of Taoism
Sex, Health, and Long Life: Manuals of
    Taoist Practice
The Taoist I Ching
Taoist Meditation
Vitality, Energy, Spirit
Wen-tzu: Understanding the Mysteries

THE UNDYING
LAMP OF ZEN

The Testament of Zen Master Torei

TRANSLATED AND EDITED BY

THOMAS CLEARY

SHAMBHALA
Boulder
2010

Shambhala Publications, Inc.
4720 Walnut Street
Boulder, Colorado 80301
www.shambhala.com

Printed in the United States of America

∞ This edition is printed on acid-free paper that meets the
American National Standards Institute z39.48 Standard.
♲ Shambhala Publications makes every effort to print on recycled paper.
For more information please visit www.shambhala.com.

Distributed in the United States by Penguin Random House LLC
and in Canada by Random House of Canada Ltd

Library of Congress Cataloging-in-Publication Data

Torei, 1721–1792.
[Shumon mujintoron. English]
The undying lamp of Zen: the testament of Zen master Torei/translated
and edited by Thomas Cleary.—1st ed.
p. cm.
Includes bibliographical references.
ISBN 978-1-59030-792-2 (pbk.: alk. paper)
1. Zen Buddhism—Doctrines—Early works to 1800. 2. Rinzai (Sect)—
Doctrines—Early works to 1800. I. Cleary, Thomas F., 1949– II.
Title.
BQ9268.T67313 2010
294.3'927—dc22
2010008666

CONTENTS

TRANSLATOR'S INTRODUCTION

The Undying Lamp of Zen is a testament of one of the most eminent Zen masters of premodern Japan, Torei Enji (1721–92), written in anticipation of his imminent death. Because of the circumstances of its composition, it is an exceptionally explicit statement of Zen Buddhist doctrine and practice.

Torei became a monk at an early age and studied Zen under the guidance of several teachers, including Kogetsu (1667–1751), a distinguished master of the Rinzai sect of Zen. Torei first met Kogetsu when he was only five years old, but the personality of this master already inspired his interest in Zen even at this early age. Ordained at the age of nine, Torei went traveling for study when he was eighteen. After some experience of Zen, on the advice of Kogetsu he called on the redoubtable Hakuin (1685–1768), a towering figure who revitalized Rinzai Zen, particularly the study of the Zen koan.

Hakuin had many enlightened disciples, but Torei is traditionally accorded special status as one of two *shinsoku* or "genius assistants" of Hakuin. Torei was responsible for much of the advanced work of Hakuin's later disciples and also contributed considerably to the systematization of Hakuin's Zen teaching.

After his Zen enlightenment was tested and acknowledged by the notoriously rigorous Hakuin, Torei's physical health broke down repeatedly, ultimately to a point where he was pronounced incurable by physicians. As he himself explains in his own preface, this was when and why he wrote *The Undying Lamp of Zen*.[1] At the time he was barely thirty years old.

The Undying Lamp of Zen affords a rare glimpse into the school of Hakuin as it was in the master's own time, conveying the intensity and fervor of revival as well as the practical precision of technical expertise. Insisting on the experience of enlightenment, and then even more on progressive practice after enlightenment, Torei provides accessible methods for both parts of the process.

Teaching Zen according to Ekayana "One Vehicle" Buddhist principles, and in answer to the needs of his own time, Torei shows how to reunify the diverse Buddhist schools experientially while retaining the advantages of their specializations. Torei also reconciles Buddhism with the other religions and philosophies of his culture—another Ekayana practice—in this case Shinto, Confucianism, and Taoism.

As it was intended to be a final testament, *The Undying Lamp of Zen* represents a range of principles and practices rarely found assembled in one place, from the most elementary to the most advanced. It is an indispensable aid to the practice of Rinzai Zen, while also providing tested traditional techniques for public access to Zen experience.

In a further sense, this treatise is a testimony to the power of vowing, an essential ingredient of Torei's teaching and practice, by which he recovered and unleashed the massive willpower and expansive energy that would heal him and propel him for another forty years of dedication, to be diffused throughout the school even after his death.

The founding of the Japanese Zen lineage to which Hakuin and Torei refer their spiritual heritage is traced back to Daio

---

1. *Shumon mujinito ron. Shumon* is a word traditionally used for Zen schools; it derives from a term in the *Lankavatara-sutra*, one of the scriptural sources of Zen, distinguishing two forms of communication and understanding: through the source (*shu*) and through explanation (*setsu*). *Mujin* means "endless," "inexhaustible," and so on; here, used to qualify the "lamp" of Zen, *undying* is chosen in respect to the testamentary nature of the work, as something transcending the author's anticipated untimely death, and his duty to pass on the light of Zen.

(1235–1308), who learned his Zen in Song-dynasty China. Hakuin's branch of this lineage became obscure in the sixteenth century, with nothing being known of a number of the masters save their names. This changed with the emergence of Master Gudo (1577–1661) as the teacher of the emperor. Very little is known of Gudo's work, but he acknowledged numerous spiritual successors. One among them, a barely literate layman, left home in his fifties after having practiced Zen under Gudo's tutelage for thirty years. This was Munan (1603–76), who would become the spiritual grandfather of Hakuin and the ancestor of modern Rinzai Zen.

Munan left a relatively rich record in simple vernacular, providing explicit instructions in the essential processes of Zen. The pivotal issues that preoccupied Hakuin and Torei in their efforts to revitalize Zen can already be seen in the work of Munan. He was a layman for most of his life, and when he left home and became a monk, even though he was a recognized successor of a national teacher (a title for teachers of emperors), he had nothing to do with monastic careerism but lived a life of simple austerity, sustained by richness of spirituality.

Munan's teachings place great emphasis on the realization of satori, or Zen enlightenment. This is a common characteristic of Rinzai Zen, but the emphasis becomes particularly marked under certain historical conditions, and also particular psychological conditions, even to the point where satori may be taken to be an end, rather than a means. In response to this trend, Munan also stressed the pitfalls in overestimating satori, and the consequent importance of maturation and development in the aftermath of the awakening experience. This concerted attention to the special requirements of each phase of Zen practice was to continue in Munan's lineage, becoming particularly prominent in the work of Hakuin, and even more so in the teaching of Torei. According to Munan:

> Satori is the eye of Buddha, the marrow of Buddha, direct enlightenment and great comfort; everything seems fine. But as wonderful as it is, satori is a great enemy of Buddha;

do not doubt. When detached from all things by satori, if there is any knowing subject at all, in a state where one is unconstrained by anything, one will act willfully, even killing parents and rulers. Thus the enemy of Buddha is satori.

The Chinese Zen Master Baizhang cautioned, "If one should say, 'I am capable of explaining, I am able to understand—I am the teacher, you are the disciple,' this is the same as demonic suggestion." Munan said, "Even if your perception of nothingness is certain, personal faults emerge, like clouds blocking the sun and moon. One must purge oneself of faults day and night."

Therefore, the mystical and moral dimensions of experience were tightly woven together in this line of Zen. Again the master Munan sums this up in a characteristically pragmatic manner, foreshadowing the persistent emphasis found in the later works of his spiritual descendants Hakuin and Torei:

> Although our school considers satori in particular to be fundamental, that doesn't necessarily mean you're finished once you've realized satori. It is imperative to cultivate conduct according to the teaching to complete the path. "According to the teaching" means knowing your basic mind as it really is. "Cultivating conduct" means using accurate insight and knowledge to eliminate obstacles of ingrained habit. This is why it is considered comparatively easy to awaken to the Way, while practicing it in action is most difficult. Therefore Bodhidharma, the great teacher, said, "Those who know the Way are many; those who practice the Way are few." Just kill your body with a diamond sword; when this body perishes, you will not fail to attain great liberation and great freedom.

The analogy of satori to a diamond sword highlights the role of enlightenment as a means of human liberation and development rather than the end thereof, while at the same time underscoring the importance of a means that is really effective, thus leading back to refinement of satori. This mutual reinforcement of satori and character development is concisely illustrated in one of the recorded conversations of Munan, wherein someone asked him about the deterioration of Buddhism. He said,

> It's quite difficult to express in words. To call yourself a renunciant because you shave your head disgraces the very name. This is a serious matter. Even if you leave your ordinary home and live under a tree or on a rock with a couple of changes of clothing and one bowl, it would be hard to say you're a real renunciant.
>
> What a real renunciant seeks is this: Our bodies have eighty-four thousand ills, the chief among them being sexual desire, desire for gain, birth and death, jealousy and envy, and reputation and advantage. Normally these are hard to control. Using satori day and night to destroy the body's ills one by one, we should become pure.
>
> "Satori" means the basic mind. Accurately recognizing the right and wrong and good and bad of things, getting rid of what's wrong while preserving and safeguarding what's right, regularly sitting to meditate to help realization of reality, if we strive to get rid of evil and continue this effort over the years, our minds will become peaceful.

Munan's designated successor Dokyo Etan (1642–1721) is a relatively obscure figure who is mostly known from the stories of Hakuin. When he was an adolescent, a Zen elder visiting his father's establishment was asked by attendant samurai to write out the name of the bodhisattva of compassion as talismans for them. When the youth also asked for one, the Zen elder refused, telling him he had the bodhisattva within him and shouldn't seek outside. The boy became absorbed in wondering about this bodhisattva within, even to the point of distraction.

This went on for several years, until he became so absorbed in this introspection that he forgot himself while climbing a ladder one day, fell off, and was knocked unconscious on hitting the ground. He then experienced satori the moment he regained consciousness. For another three years he sought out Buddhist teachers to gain perspective on his experience. Then he met Zen Master Munan when he traveled to the capital with his father at the age of nineteen. After a severe apprenticeship with Munan and acknowledgment as his spiritual successor, Etan took on no monastic office but remained a recluse all his life.

In Hakuin's lineage, Etan is referred to as Shoju Rojin, the Old Man of True Perception, after the name of his hermitage. In Buddhist Sino-Japanese, *shoju* is really a technical term, a translation of the Sanskrit *samadhi*, concentration or absorption. Although his interactions with Hakuin are typically represented as mediated by clusters of Zen koans, Shoju's essential practice is referred to as continuity of right mindfulness, and his epithet evokes his lifelong devotion to perfecting this practice. According to a commemorative poem attributed to him, nonetheless, it was not until he was more than fifty years old that he finally attained unbroken continuity. This element of long-term effort in Shoju's story plays an important role in the school of Hakuin, as noted by Torei, to emphasize cultivation and maturation after enlightenment. Hakuin himself illustrates this point emphatically in a letter to a Zen elder:

> There's nothing without a beginning, but those who can achieve an end are rare. People in Zen schools start out with admirable will and respectable conduct, but when they come to have a roof over their heads and cold and warmth are up to them, fame and profit are sweet as sugar while focus on Zen is bitter as yellow plum. Growing slacker and more negligent with the passing days and months, they wind up becoming a bunch of maggots. Facing old age will be a bellyful of sadness.
>
> Looking for those who are capable of starting and who also complete the end, you can count them on your fingers. I happen to be one of them. Abbacy is indeed something to be careful about and wary of. Recently I have heard you retired. That's delightful, but regrettable, because Zen is not

something that you stop when you have understood and discard when you have realized. The more you understand, the more you study. The more you realize, the more you take up. This is called the unfinished case.

Don't let the frequency and complication of worldly duties stymie you; don't prefer to sit as if dead in a peaceful, quiet place. Whether walking, sitting, standing, or lying down, earnestly keep it carefully—where do you lose it, where do you not lose it? This is a predecessor's way of focus on Zen.

Now you are letting a defeated general expound military matters. It seems somewhat shameful. Nevertheless, the overturned car ahead may be a safeguard for the cars behind.

In Torei's conception of devotion to perpetual practice, emerging from his own experiences and vigorously reinforced by the teaching heritage of Munan, Shoju, and Hakuin, time is not only quantitative and referential, but particularly qualitative and experiential. Persistence thus becomes meaningful only in the context of procedural efficiency. Torei explains this principle of timing in Zen practice with the analogy of the four seasons in an interesting letter to a layman who has already realized satori:

Overall, in practice timing is of prime importance. If you don't know the timing, you waste effort and diminish your own spiritual strength.

It is like plowing in spring, weeding in summer, harvesting in autumn, and conserving in winter. Your spring plowing work is done, and your seedlings of seeing nature have grown healthy. From now the summer season is most important, just transplanting to the fields of totality, and weeding. Everything else should be deferred to autumn and winter.

The "fields of totality" means transferring that solidly empowered great meditation concentration into the midst of both pleasant and unpleasant situations, activity and quietude, sorrow and joy. "Weeding" means seeing through good thoughts and bad thoughts, confusion and clarity, whenever they occur, perfecting the great potential beyond things, becoming like a fine sword.

Other than this, the ancient examples, official decisions [koan], and so on, should by all means be put off for now. One of the ancients was even made to sleep for three days and three nights because when the joy of empowerment is extreme, it then damages your faculties for the Way. There was also a famous teacher who wrote the words *retreat of silence* with instructions to keep to them for three years. The ancient worthies of the Soto sect of Zen would have students cultivate absorption in the relative and absolute for three years after seeing nature. Absorption in the relative and absolute is what I call summer practice.

In sum, the ancient worthies, each in their own way, calmly cultivated practice gradually, from the fundamental. That being said, if you investigate ancient examples and so on at this juncture, when some commotion occurs in the chest with a sense of joy, then you flounder around and faculties for the Way are naturally lost. It's as if one were intending to teach various arts and crafts to children, and wound up smacking them around and beating them to death.

This is a most essential point for practitioners. If you violate this strict regulation, you are no colleague of mine.

As *The Undying Lamp of Zen* illustrates, the matter of timing underlies systematic organization of Buddhist scriptures in terms of phases of personal development and responsive education. The understanding of time in terms of mental states and experiences also explains the Zen emphasis on individual prescription for maximum efficiency of teachings and practices. For this reason, Torei's methodology includes extensive outreach and accommodation as well as intensive rigor and exclusion. This treatise therefore includes a wide range of Zen Buddhist teaching, from the most open and accessible to the most arcane and esoteric, enabling everyone from the absolute beginner to the advanced practitioner to benefit from its encouragement and instruction.

THE UNDYING LAMP OF ZEN

PREFACE

If you want to read this treatise, do so from start to finish, thoroughly penetrating each point. Don't just pick out a saying or a chapter that conforms to your own liking and consider that right.

First, distinguish the source of our school, which has its special significance.

Next, know about faith and practice.

Third, distinguish the mistakes of small knowledge and small views.

Fourth, it is necessary to know that seeing nature really and truly is all in great doubt and great faith, and no intellectual discrimination is applicable—when the time comes, it occurs naturally. This realm is the root of the substance of the whole treatise. The phenomenon of seeing nature is easy to clarify but difficult to use thoroughly in both action and repose, in both adverse and favorable circumstances. Please focus even more intently when you get here, for otherwise the verbal teachings of the Buddhas and Masters will all come down to mere words and won't be real, living methods. When you have truly developed a foothold, continuously mindful, present in all situations, only then can you penetrate sayings.

Fifth, always test everyday application, valuing only continuity of right mindfulness. Application of practice varies in depth and refinement; these distinctions are most difficult to discern. To find out about them, carefully examine the sayings of Buddhas and Masters; you absolutely have to think of their subtle points. This is called the eye that penetrates barriers.

Sixth, after having gotten through the locks of the Buddhas and Masters one by one, deeply believe there is an experience beyond Buddhas and Masters, and cultivate more and more, practice more and more, don't even think of retreat. This matter is by no means easy. Just look into reality in yourself; search into the impenetrable stories of the ancients over and over—the essential message transmitted by the Zen masters lies hidden herein. Even so, if not for the training of an enlightened teacher, how can you gain any results?

Seventh, depending on the depth of insight and the degree of expertise in application, there are enormous differences in the power and function released. This is the reason why people with the same views and the same practices, now as of old, have differences in their virtues.

Eighth, what is received from the teacher, inspiring gratitude for the teaching, is something you should not turn your back on, even at the expense of your life. When you include gratitude for the achievements of successive generations of Zen masters, each one equal, no amount of effort is adequate to requite it. Only by producing one or two genuine successors can you requite any of that debt.

Ninth, whether concealed in a forest or concealed in a city, in all events and all places, just consider development of primary importance; don't be pulled by confusing focus on things of the world, but regard the ancients' models of attentiveness.

Tenth, "circulation" means the whole process of cultivation and practice. At first you develop determination based on this, then cultivate practice based on this, seek the subtleties of differentiation based on this, make a life beyond convention based on this, grip the claws and fangs of the cave of the teaching, and wear the miraculous life-taking talisman.

With unobstructed, fluid, independent spiritual capacities you enter into the coarse as well as the fine, into the real as well as the conventional, to produce one or two genuine successors, to create a perpetual lamp lighting the world. The superabundance of light diffuses to everyone, bringing benefit without end, making all forms of life your dwelling place lifetime after lifetime, generation after generation, independently liberated, freely bestowing benefit.

All of this is produced by repeated training and refinement of this subtlety beyond convention, cultivated after realization. Only with such faith and resolution, such development and maturation, can you be called a Buddhist.

After my perception was fully developed, I had not yet mastered the ancients' subtleties of differentiation, so I stayed in seclusion for more than one hundred days of intense cultivation.

A sense of shame and determination penetrated my bones and marrow. Though I'd attained my aim, because I hadn't taken care of my physical health and had overexerted my mind, my internal organs were all stressed, resulting in serious illness.

Subsequently, though I relaxed to take care of this, it was by no means easy to cure. I was subjected to mischief from outside, or troubled by worldly relations, and suffered the sickbed three times; once I'd get well, I'd fall sick again. This went on for three years. The doctors gave up on me, telling me that even if I recovered from this illness for the time being, I couldn't have more than three or four years left to live.

At this point I reflected that my life was not worth regretting. I only lamented the fact that I had not yet fulfilled my original vow to help myself and help others, and had gone through all this hardship in vain.

Finally I emulated Canonical Master Seng Zhao,[1] who wrote a treatise as he was awaiting execution, and hurriedly set forth this exposition. Sitting on a cushion day and night with writing materials by my side, I wrote down what came to me, completing a manuscript in only thirty days. I call it "Discourse on the Undying Lamp of Zen." This is based on the sense of one lamp imparting its flame to hundreds and thousands of lamps, in an undying succession of lights.

After this I sat and reclined at ease, leaving my life to fate.

---

1. Seng Zhao (374–414) was a disciple of the famous translator Kumarajiva. See *The Blue Cliff Record*, case 40.

Then I felt the illness getting lighter and lighter day by day. After another half year, I knew in myself that I could survive.

For this reason I reconsidered—had my illness been terminal and had I presented this treatise to my old teacher [Hakuin], I would have asked that he make any useful points of enduring encouragement for later people, and if it had nothing useful in it I'd consign it to the fire. Now that I had been able to get over this illness, with the living person present what would be the use of dead complications?

At this point I was going to burn my treatise, but before I had done so my old teacher personally sent me a letter, and I went back to see him. As we spoke in private, I mentioned this treatise and eventually read it to the old teacher. He said it could be a help to younger students, and firmly forbade me to burn it.

This being so, I nevertheless kept it stored away for a long time. Now, due to the urgent request of believers, I cannot but permit it to be copied.

However, writings and sayings are a basis of liberation and a basis of bondage too. If given to the wrong person, or at the wrong time, even ghee turns to poison. I beg you to reflect deeply upon this and not let this treatise be read by the wrong people or at the wrong time. If you violate this strict rule, you are no comrade of mine, ever. Especially since I have been sick a lot and unable to edit and correct the manuscript, how could this text be considered definitive? It will only be suitable as a definitive text after I've had a chance to recheck it sometime.

TOREI ENJI, 1751

The Source of Zen

When the Great Enlightened World-Honored One was first born, he walked seven steps in all directions, pointed to the sky with one hand and pointed to the earth with the other hand, and said with the roar of a lion, "In the heavens above and on earth below, only I am honored." Tsk! He wound up revealing an experience. Yunmen said, "If I had seen him at that time, I would have killed him with one stroke of my cane and fed his flesh to the dogs, so that the world might be at peace."

Ying-an brought this up and said:

This is a speck of poison brought down at birth; Yunmen is affected by it, so he knows what it comes down to and brings it up and uses it appropriately. If this were all there was to it, Buddha's teaching would have died out; so he wound up demonstrating a model of it—leaving home to practice austerities, then going into the Himalaya Mountains and sitting straight for six years, then suddenly realizing great enlightenment one night, whereupon he exclaimed, "How wonderful! All living beings have inherent in them the knowledge and virtues of those who arrive at reality!"

It is also said that once the Buddha attained enlightenment he contemplated the universe and saw that the plants, trees, and lands all attain buddhahood. True enough, but what a pity! The principles he realized and the states he experienced, though not within the reach of language, were provisionally collected—this is called the *Avatamsaka-sutra*. The fundamental cycle of teaching, the discourses of the Buddha's whole lifetime, all repose therein. Only those of superior faculties can understand it, while the mediocre and lesser are not up to it. This is why Buddha taught the four truths at the Deer Park, and next he explained the twelve causes and conditions and the six perfections.[1] These are called the three vehicles.

Because of doctrinal imbalance and inferiority of aspiration and practice, Buddha also expounded teaching with balancing reprobation to break through this limitation, comparing the two vehicles to mangy foxes.[2] The intention was to get students of the canon to change their attitudes to universality and take to the Fundamental Vehicle. Thus there is a Great Vehicle with distinguishing doctrine; when those in the two vehicles hear it, they lose their will, while bodhisattvas go ahead and find out its meaning. Therefore the *Sutra of Vimalakirti* says, "When all the disciples hear this teaching of inconceivable liberation, the sound of their wail will shake the universe. All bodhisattvas will joyfully accept this teaching."

Later, Buddha repeatedly expounded the teaching of insight, the purifying principle of emptiness in which the two vehicles and three vehicles, higher and lower, are mixed. This is what is referred to as leading from small emptiness into great emptiness, breaking down false emptiness to attain true emptiness.[3]

After many years like this, when the time came and the effect ripened, Buddha abruptly articulated the complete all-at-once teaching of the characteristics of reality. He simply doused them

1. See *The Flower Ornament Scripture*, book 8, for a comprehensive treatment of the four truths; *The Flower Ornament Scripture*, pp. 745–48, for the twelve causes and conditions; and *Buddhist Yoga*, pp. 75–76, for the six perfections.

2. "The two vehicles" refers to systems based on the four truths and twelve conditions, whose goal is nirvana or individual liberation. The negativity associated with this term is in reference to the relative narrowness of this goal in comparison to that of the bodhisattva, who strives for complete enlightenment for self and others.

3. Those in the two lesser vehicles contemplate emptiness of person, while those in the third vehicle, the bodhisattvas, contemplate emptiness of both person and phenomena.

with foul water, and the three vehicles and five natures equally entered into the One Vehicle of Buddhahood.[4] But even so, they entered by faith, not their own knowledge, so they received predictions for the future and were not said to be Buddhas immediately. He just wanted them to have the same faith and practice as the *Avatamsaka-sutra* and the same realization and penetration as the *Nirvana-sutra*.[5]

Tremendous! Buddha's teaching is very deep, hard to fully comprehend. The teacher is the Tamer of Humanity with Ten Powers, the students are savants and sages, so how could the teachings be superficial! His inductive guidance was also subtle, so every individual realized unaffected true nature; each one was stabilized in acceptance of reality without regression.

This being so, even having done all this, he nevertheless also had something beyond. At the very end, one day at an assembly on Spirit Mountain he held up a flower to the congregation. No one in the immense crowd knew what to make of this, except the reverend Kasyapa, who broke out in a smile. The Buddha said, "I have the treasury of the eye of truth, the subtle mind of nirvana, the formless teaching of reality; I entrust this to Elder Kasyapa."

This is why our school has a distinct life. The special transmission outside of doctrine didn't come about arbitrarily.

Brahma went to Spirit Mountain, presented a gold flower to Buddha, then sacrificed his body to be a chair, pleading that Buddha expound the truth to the multitudes. Buddha sat on the seat and held up the flower; no one, people or deities, knew what to make of this. There was a golden-faced ascetic who alone broke into a smile. The World-Honored One said, "I have this treasury of the eye of truth, which I entrust to Elder Kasyapa. Keep it well."

Later Ananda asked Reverend Kasyapa, "Besides the golden-sleeved robe the Buddha bequeathed to you, what did he transmit?"

---

4. The "five natures" refer to the psychologies associated with the three vehicles, plus those of indefinite nature and those with no such nature.

5. This refers to the *Mahaparinirvana-sutra* of the Mahayana, the *Scripture of the Great Demise*, not the Pali *Nibbana-sutta*.

Kasyapa called to Ananda; Ananda immediately responded. Kasyapa said, "Take down the flagpole at the entrance." At these words Ananda was greatly enlightened.[6]

From then on it was transmitted successively, third to Sonavasa, fourth to Upagupta, fifth Tirthika, sixth Micchaka, seventh Vasumitra, eighth Buddhanandi, ninth Punyamitra, tenth Venerable Parsva. Next was Punyayasas, next Asvaghosa, next Kapimala, next the *mahasattva* Nagarjuna, next Kanadeva, next Rahulata, next Sanghanandi, next Jayasata, next Kumarata, twentieth Jayata, next Vasubandhu, next Venerable Manora, next Haklena. The twenty-fourth, Sinha, transmitted the eye of truth to Vaisasita, and the robe of faith and verse of teaching were even fresher after the firewood had burned out.[7] Next was Punyamitra, next Prajnatara, and with the twenty-eighth transmission it reached Bodhidharma, who made his way to China, and simply passed on the seal of the enlightened mind, showing this manner of a wearer of the patchwork robe for nine years on Few Houses Peak of Mount Song.

The second patriarch, Great Teacher Ke, bowed three times and stood in place. At first he cut off his arm and awakened; later he got the marrow and received the robe.[8]

The third patriarch was named Sengcan. The fourth patriarch was named Daoxin. Coming to the fifth patriarch, Hongren, southern and northern schools divided sudden and gradual. The sixth generation to transmit the robe was Huineng, who was capable of enlightened work by virtue of wisdom, originally illiterate and still not understanding "Buddhism."[9]

---

6. For an interpretation of this story and the succession stories of the masters whose names follow, see *Transmission of Light*.

7. Sinha was put to death by an anti-Buddhist king; the firewood refers to his cremation.

8. See *Transmission of Light* for these stories about the second patriarch.

9. A classic Zen saying has it that Huineng received the robe signifying transmission of Zen mastery because he didn't understand Buddhism, he only understood the path. This means he didn't understand doctrine as an intellectual object, but as a guide to practice. See *The Sutra of Hui-neng: Grand Master of Zen*.

On Nanyue there was Huairang; at Qingyuan there was
Xingsi: From Jiangxi and Hunan their descendants filled the
land.[10] The golden rooster's single grain of millet, no separate
road in China; the colt that was sent forth trampled everyone
on earth to death.[11] Master Baizhang made a representation
then set it aside, and he was deafened for three days. Huangbo,
hearing of this, stuck out his tongue.[12] Jiangxi had established
the way of the school; Linji was the Vajra King, applying illumination and function at the same time; who would have known
the true eye of the teaching would perish in a blind ass?[13] Xinghua's pinch of incense worked hard to protect his posterity.[14]
Nanyuan's patience under the cane didn't defer to his teacher
when it was time to act.[15] Fengxue's cat was fierce, brought up
to get rid of vermin.[16] The method of security up in a tree was

---

10. Nanyue, or Southern Peak, is the epithet of the southernmost of the five
sacred mountains of China. Many Buddhists and Taoists lived there. For
Huairang (677–744) and his famous disciple Mazu (709–88), who is here referred to as Jiangxi after the region where he taught, see *The Blue Cliff Record*,
pp. 566–67. For Mazu's teaching, see *Teachings of Zen*, pp. 7–11. For Xingsi of
Qingyuan (660–740), see *Book of Serenity*, case 5. Hunan, also a place name,
here refers to Xingsi's great disciple Shitou (700–790). For Shitou's teaching,
see *Timeless Spring*. Mazu and Shitou were referred to in their time as the Two
Doors of Immortality, and most of the classical Zen masters descended from
their schools.

11. "The golden rooster's grain of millet" refers to a prediction by Prajnatara,
the teacher of Bodhidharma, who brought Zen to China; the colt sent forth
refers to a prediction by Huineng (638–713), the teacher of Huairang, about
Mazu, whose surname means "horse."

12. See *The Blue Cliff Record*, cases 11 and 53.

13. *Linji* is pronounced *Rinzai* in Japanese; Rinzai Zen is named after the master Linji (d. 867). See *The Blue Cliff Record*, pp. 590–94; "Zen Master Linji"
in *Zen Essence*; and "The House of Lin-chi" in *The Five Houses of Zen*. The
"blind ass" refers to Linji's successor Sansheng (n.d.), who compiled the classic
Linji lu (Record of Linji). For this story, see *Book of Serenity*, case 13.

14. Xinghua (830–88) is reckoned a successor of Linji. The "pinch of incense"
refers to respect.

15. Nanyuan (860–930) was a successor to Xinghua. See *The Blue Cliff Record*,
commentary to case 38, for this allusion.

16. Fengxue (896–973) succeeded Nanyuan. See *The Blue Cliff Record*, cases
38 and 61.

not to be granted to a brother-in-law.[17] What was the right thing to say? Shoushan abruptly left. Fenyang, the lion of the West River, picked up a cane and chased Ciming, whose attainment was beyond ordinary sense, as he stuck his thigh with an awl to continue the way of the school.[18]

Yangqi's thorn-ball, only Baiyun took up and held.[19] The Yellow Crane Pavilion with one punch, Parrot Island with one kick, more spirited than spirited, stylish among the stylish, once Master Yan bit through, a hundred flavors were all there.[20] Breaking out in a sweat all over, he established the way of East Mountain on a grand scale.[21] Yuanwu watched his step, and he alone annihilated our school.[22] Huqiu saved some money but still had claws and fangs besides.[23] With Ying-an's hammer to the back of the brain, happily a healthy pulse came through.[24] Mi-an's broken bowl of sand slept in peace at Miaoxi; the robe of transmission wound up at Songyuan.[25] With black beans on the right

17. This alludes to a verse by Fenyang (947–1024), successor to Fengxue's successor Shoushan (926–93), mentioned next in this list. For Fenyang's teaching, see "Zen Master Fenyang" in *Zen Lessons*; and *The Blue Cliff Record*, pp. 638–41.

18. Ciming (986–1039) was Fenyang's successor. He used to keep himself awake during meditation vigils by sticking himself with an awl.

19. Yangqi (992–1049) succeeded Fenyang. Baiyun (1025–72) succeeded Yangqi. For teachings of Yangqi, see "Zen Master Yangqi" in *Zen Essence*. For Baiyun, see *Zen Lessons*, cases 29–33.

20. Master Yan is Wuzu Fayan (1024–1104), successor of Baiyun. See *Zen Lessons*, cases 18–28; "Zen Master Wuzu" in *Zen Essence*; and *Unlocking the Zen Koan*, case 45.

21. Wuzu's school was called the East Mountain school after its location.

22. Yuanwu (1083–1135) succeeded Wuzu. Yuanwu is the commentator of the classic *The Blue Cliff Record*. For Yuanwu's letters, see *Zen Letters*. See also *Zen Lessons*, cases 80–87; "Zen Master Yuanwu" in *Zen Essence*; and "Yuanwu, *Essentials of Mind*" in "The House of Lin-chi," *The Five Houses of Zen*.

23. Huqiu (1077–1136) succeeded Yuanwu.

24. Ying-an (d. 1163) succeeded Huqiu. See "Zen Master Ying-an" in *Zen Lessons*; and *The Pocket Zen Reader*, pp. 76, 83–89, 92–93, 131–32, 157–59.

25. For Mi-an, see "Zen Master Mi-an" in *Zen Essence*. "Miaoxi" refers to Dahui (1069–1163), a successor of Yuanwu, who was called a second coming of Linji; see "Zen Master Dahui" in *Zen Essence*, and *Zen Lessons*, cases 145–49; Dahui's famous letters are translated by J. C. Cleary in *Swampland Flowers*. Songyuan (1139–1209) studied with Ying-an and Dahui, but finally succeeded Mi-an.

road, Yun-an's capacity to take away the robe was handed right to Xutang.[26]

I bow my head to Master Daio, first patriarch of the Eastern Sea [Japan]. He journeyed twice, and the proliferation of his progeny was foretold. The razorlike sword of Murasakino, sharpened for twenty years, cut off the hands and feet of Buddhas and Patriarchs, then was taken by Kanzan, who declared the oak tree to have a thief's potential.[27] Dealing solely with the transcendental, he refined it for thirty autumns and found one individual, Juo.[28] Muin's stability was a great eye for the whole world; he managed to snatch the jet-black dragon's pearl.[29] Nippo illuminated past and present; the way of his school reached Giten.[30] The teaching was lofty and its operation even stricter. The apricot of Mount Heng bore poison fruit; intense effort was made to master the two marvels; black beans were mixed with an accurate eye to irritate the intestines of four heirs.[31]

26. "Black beans" is Zen slang for written words; to have "black beans on the right road" means to master both Zen and the canonical teachings. Yun-an (1156–1226) succeeded Songyuan; Xutang (1185–1269) succeeded Yun-an. Xutang was the teacher of the Japanese National Teacher Daio, who traveled to China to study and brought this lineage of Zen to Japan; see "National Teacher Daio's Letters to Meditators" in *The Original Face*.

27. "The razorlike sword of Murasakino" refers to Daio's successor Daito (1282–1337), whose successor in turn was Kanzan (1277–1360); all three of these masters were designated "national teachers," a title for teachers of emperors, and this lineage is referred to by the second syllables of their honorific names, as the O-To-Kan school of Zen. Kanzan's teaching is only known by a single verse, on the ancient story in which a student asks a famous master the living meaning of Zen, and the master replies, "The oak tree in the garden"; to say this has "a thief's potential" is a warning not to let the mirrorlike perception of being-as-is turn into absorption in objects.

28. Juo Sohitsu (1296–1380), successor of Kanzan.

29. Muin Soin (1326–1410) succeeded Juo Sohitsu.

30. Nippo Soshun (1368–1448) succeeded Muin; he was succeeded by Giten Gensho (1393–1462).

31. "The apricot of Mount Heng" refers to the ancestral school of Zen in China. The term "the two marvels" comes from the Tendai school, describing the *Hokke* or *Lotus-sutra*; "the two marvels" are relative and absolute: As it is introduced to broaden minds, the teaching of the Lotus is called marvelous in comparison to the teachings that preceded it; this is the relative marvel. As it

Toyo's natural capacity, with an inexhaustible treasury of icy medicinal fruit, blew in the springtime of Taiga, with the fragrances of a hundred flowers coming on in clouds; his teaching methods were uncompromisingly strict, while his bones of vows protected his progeny.[32]

Koho's novelty was prominent, avoiding discussion gone off into the wilds.[33] Sensho was made of iron, going through years of harsh treatment; Ian's fierce personality had the spirit of sitting through seven cushions; Tozen was exceptional in his practice.[34] The sun rose in the morning sky and at day's end hid in a middling mountain.[35] Revealing half his body in empty space, he despised the easy approval found everywhere. His resentment put the onus on one heir: of twenty-four schools, most lost their transmission, but the descendants of old Gudo of Kanzan still exist today.[36]

Munan's three-foot sword killed completely, not leaving a

---

absorbs the other teachings into a total unity, there is no more comparison; this is called the absolute marvel. "Black beans mixed with an accurate eye," like an earlier analogue of this expression, refers to combined mastery of Zen and the canonical teachings, such as the preceding allusion to the study of Tendai teachings. "Four heirs" refers to four successors of the last mentioned Master Giten, among whom was the next mentioned, Toyo Eicho (1428–1504).

32. Taiga is Zen Master Taiga Tankyo (n.d.).

33. Koho is Zen Master Koho Genkun (n.d.).

34. Sensho is Zen Master Zensho Zuisho (n.d.). Ian is Zen Master Ian Chisatsu (n.d.); the description of his spirit refers to a famous Chinese master who sat in meditation so long he wore out seven cushions before he attained enlightenment. Tozen is Zen Master Tozen Soshin. (He has been identified with Sekko Soshin [1408–86], but this is problematic. The latter was a successor of Muin Soin [1326–1410], an earlier figure in the lineage.)

35. This means Zen Master Yozan Keiyo (1559–1629). The reference to "day's end" alludes to the waning of Zen to near extinction, and the hiding of the sun alludes to the obscurity of this Zen master.

36. Gudo Toshoku (1577–1661) succeeded Yozan. The reference to the "twenty-four schools" is an allusion to a famous verse by Gudo himself, on taking up the abbacy of Myoshinji, suggesting that his was the only one of twenty-four original Zen lineages in Japan to survive.

body; Shoju wrested it away and polished it for forty years.[37] His secret room was airtight; he cut out the subtleties of Buddhas and Patriarchs. He arrested our Kokurin, whose whole body suffered poisonous pains.[38] Without you, sectarian style favoring propagation would have burdened descendants forever—where would your angry scolding ever cease?[39] In order to resolve your doubts about this, I have listed teachers of authentic succession. I have no way of knowing about the doctrines inherited elsewhere.[40]

QUESTION: If even the million savants and sages of Buddha's time couldn't understand, and only Kasyapa broke into a smile, why did so many understand after Buddha's extinction?

ANSWER: Those who entered by way of doctrinal vehicles had a lot of intellectual obstructions, which stuck to their skin and adhered to their bones, so they could not experience liberation. Those who entered through Zen never set up intellectual objects, so as soon as they applied it in practice it was easy to detach from intellectual objects.

QUESTION: Then why didn't Buddha teach Zen first, instead of expounding so many doctrinal vehicles?

ANSWER: When the Buddha first emerged in the world, people's

37. Munan (1603–76), one of Gudo's many successors, was a samurai and in his teaching often used metaphors of the sword, killing, and annihilating the body to represent Zen transcendence; he studied Zen as a layman for thirty years, then left home and became a monk at the age of fifty-two. "Shoju" means "accurate perception" and is a Buddhist technical term for correct *samadhi,* commonly translated as "concentration" or "absorption"; this was the name of the hermitage where Munan's spiritual successor Dokyo Etan (1642–1721) lived, and it is also the epithet by which he is commonly called, Shoju Rojin, the latter component meaning "old man."

38. Kokurin is Zen Master Hakuin (1685–1768), regarded as the reviver of Rinzai Zen, from whom all modern Rinzai lineages claim descent. Hakuin recounts harsh treatment at the hands of Shoju, and he made himself seriously ill by overexertion, as also did the author of this treatise, himself one of Hakuin's disciples. The "you" in what follows refers to Hakuin.

39. "Propagation" means emphasis on doctrine rather than enlightenment.

40. Here "your" refers to an interlocutor, thus to the reader. The recitation of lineage was a ritual that developed in Confucian cultures, but the esoteric meaning is to focus awareness on the continuum of consciousness underlying successive mental states.

faith was as yet immature, and in India there were countless other paths, each with different doctrines, and all sorts of misunderstandings. If Buddha had not expounded the doctrinal vehicles, perhaps no one would have believed. Therefore the *Lotus-sutra* says, "I reflected that if I only recommended the vehicle of buddhahood, people submerged in suffering would not be able to believe this teaching. As they will repudiate the teaching and disbelieve it, they'll fall into the three states of misery."⁴¹ Now, though Zen students don't set up a doctrinal vehicle, they first use the doctrines as objects of faith and make them bases of practice. The sutra spoken by Vimalakirti says, "Just get rid of the sickness, don't discard the teaching." Viewed in correct perspective, the five periods, eight doctrines, three vehicles, and one vehicle are equally the Zen master's single experience of progressive transcendence, with nowhere for you to stick your beak in.⁴²

QUESTION: There is a teaching called Vairocana's miraculous empowerment, treating symbolic virtues esoterically. What you

---

41. "The three states of misery" represent embodiments of the so-called three poisons of greed, aggression, and folly.

42. "The five periods" refer to five phases of Buddha's teaching as reckoned in the Tendai school: First is the Avatamsaka period, when Buddha supposedly expounded everything at once in the *Flower Ornament Scripture*; virtually no one understood, so the second period, called the Deer Park period, represents remedial teachings, the so-called Lesser Vehicle leading to nirvana; in the third period, called the Universal period, Buddha rebukes the narrowness of those who cling to nirvana and turns attention to the Greater Vehicle of universal enlightenment; the fourth period, named for the Perfection of Insight scriptures, focuses on the teaching of emptiness, eliminating attachments to dogma; the fifth period is named for the *Lotus* and *Mahaparinirvana Scriptures*, in which Buddha reveals the Dharma as an eternal reality. The eight doctrines is also a Tendai construction: The first is called the canonical doctrine, focusing on attainment of nirvana; the second is called the common doctrine, focusing on emptiness; the third is called the separate doctrine, addressed only to bodhisattvas; the fourth is called the complete doctrine, addressed to bodhisattvas of the highest faculties; the next four refer to modes of teaching—first is sudden, second gradual, third secret, and fourth indefinite. The three vehicles refer to teachings for listeners, individual illuminates, and bodhisattvas. The One Vehicle refers to the comprehensive teachings, such as found in the *Flower-Ornament* and *Lotus-sutras*.

have been pointing out reveals the great principle of shutting off feelings. How does the esoteric teaching compare to Zen?

ANSWER: The Buddha's teaching of self-experienced *samadhi* may be illustrated by metaphorical explanations, but he still feared people wouldn't understand, so he also used a very compassionate expedient in presenting these symbolic forms. So when he spoke of principle, he utterly transcended everything, and his presentation of phenomena was in mystic accord with the characteristics of reality. The embodiment of reality is considered the teacher; the teachings said to be inherent in nature are the features of the exposition. A sphere of objects is called a mandala; this is the Buddha's esoteric representation of the qualities of the body of reality by means of miraculous empowerment.

In ancient times the great Nagarjuna went to the immense iron stupa of the South, where he empowered seven white seeds and threw them at it. The door of the stupa suddenly opened, and Nagarjuna was going to enter, but the four guardian kings stopped him. He bowed and apologized, and was at last able to go inside. Then Vajrapani Bodhisattva transmitted teachings to him. Nagarjuna memorized them, and then came out and compiled them. They have been transmitted all the way to the present.

"South India" means purity of open awareness; the "iron stupa" means basic ignorance. The "seven grains" mean the seven branches of enlightenment;[43] "white" means purity. A "seed" means one moment of thought. "Empowerment" means contemplative awareness. The "opening of the stupa door" means the attainment of *samadhi.* "Obstruction by the four kings" means it is guarded on all four sides by the sense of delight in attaining something, so there is still separation from inherent nature. "Bowing and apologizing" means letting go of your body and giving up your life. "Gaining entry" means initial realization. "The Great Sun [Vairocana Buddha]" means inherent nature; esoteric teachings are the teachings present in inherent nature, so they

---

43. The "seven branches (or limbs) of enlightenment" are discernment, energy, joy, relief, relinquishment, stability, and mindfulness.

are said to be expounded spontaneously. "Vajrapani" stands for knowledge attained afterward. "Transmission" means full understanding. Memorizing means never losing it once you've attained it. "Exiting" means bodhisattvas don't stay in the state they realize; it means they help other people.

If you are able to observe the basic ignorance in the clear mind of open awareness using the pure thought of the seven branches of enlightenment, then ignorance will suddenly break apart and inherent nature will appear. At this time, because of joyfully holding on to a sense of having attained something, you can't see through your own nature. Only when you let go of gain and loss and affirmation and negation all at once do you see through your own nature. Countless teachings are evident everywhere before your eyes, but if you do not understand them by means of knowledge acquired after, you cannot know the distinct elements of the state of enlightenment.

So the ability to understand the teachings is all produced by knowledge attained afterward.[44] Once you've seen through this truth, then all your activities, even casual, are the Great Way, are all teachings. This is called the mind with secret adornments, because it is not another's experience.[45]

Later people didn't understand this and mistakenly made representational forms. If you want to master this teaching, first you need to see nature. If you want to master this teaching without seeing nature, it won't be possible. I don't say the exoteric and esoteric doctrines are all wrong, but they are only on the road discussing the subtle state of enlightenment without being able to experience it in themselves.[46] They can't even attain the reality body, let alone what is beyond the reality body. For this reason the doctrinal vehicles only discuss the near and far of the road, while Zen immediately points beyond the road. Doctrinal

---

44. That is, after realizing intrinsic nature.

45. "The mind with secret (or esoteric) adornments" is the term used for the crowning experience of Shingon Buddhism.

46. Referring to the reduction of these doctrinal schools to academic and ritual formalities.

vehicles speak remotely of attaining the subtle state of enlightenment, while Zen directly tests the truth of enlightenment.

Suppose, for example, a pauper talks about the wealth of a rich family. He may talk of it as well as can be, but he can't spend it himself. So what use is it to him? It's like commoners talking about the nobility of kings. They may talk of it as well as can be, but they are still commoners. If they want the nobility of kings or the wealth of the rich, they'd better get it themselves.

When you're seeking, you don't pay attention to the nobility of kings or the wealth of the rich, you just consider your own resources and test your own nobility. As you seek it you define it, increasing and advancing as you can. This is why progress and practice may be very different even if the intent is the same.

If you practice the instructions of the scriptures, you often linger over the tracks of the teachings—when will you experience liberation? It is like the case of a merchant who keeps the conditions under which others have made profits, yet misses opportunities himself and thus makes no profit. There are no conditions for profiting—it is the gain that is valued. It is like a general who maintains the conditions under which others have been successful, yet misses opportunities himself, and so gains no success. Success has no conditions—it is the attainment that is valued.

I don't say there are no conditions at all, just that they are not to be held to dogmatically. First find out the underlying intent, recognize what is expedient, observe changes according to the times, take or leave according to suitability. In our Zen school, we don't rely on the tracks of doctrine, but have a special aim. Dealing with people according to their potential, freely, without impediment, is also like this.

If you want to obtain all the riches of the wealthy, first you must return to the magnate of your own mind; then an inexhaustible treasury of teachings will naturally come into your hands. If you want to attain all the nobility of kings, first you must call on the king of your own mind, and unsurpassed nobility will ultimately accrue to your person.

Since ancient times there have been those among devotees of

doctrine who have understood in this way, so those who have entered by way of doctrine have not been few. Now it is not that way at all. Even though what they discuss may exhaust wonders and plumb mysteries, they repudiate the two vehicles and reject provisional vehicles; they argue over partiality versus completeness, exotericism versus esotericism. On examination, though, they cannot even attain the realizations of the two vehicles, much less bodhisattvahood—when have they ever dreamed of the One Vehicle of buddhahood? Where are the partial and complete, the exoteric and esoteric?

Our Zen school is not this way. Directly transcending expedients, meditating intensely, as soon as we get the essence, then the exoteric and esoteric teachings of Buddha all appear at once. Then we ram through a number of strong barriers, then come back and read scriptures and treatises, which now seem like we've expounded them ourselves. Afterward we raze the forest of wisdom, kick over the site of enlightenment, destroy the transcendental, and cut off the pulse of Buddhas and Patriarchs. Exoteric and esoteric—what idle fancies are these? Even the reality body and the wisdom body still have to withdraw from the universe!

[2]

FAITH AND PRACTICE

In the book on "Appearance of the Realized" in the *Flower Ornament Scripture* it says,

> The knowledge of those who arrive at reality reaches everywhere. Why? Because there is not a single being but has knowledge of those who arrive at reality; it's just that they cannot actually realize it because of the delusions and fixations of false ideas. If they would detach from false ideas, all knowledge, spontaneous knowledge, and unhindered knowledge could come to the fore. It is as if there were a scripture the size of the universe, recording everything in the universe, completely contained in an atom, and as in one atom so in all atoms. Now there is someone with clear and accurate insight who has fully developed pure clairvoyance and sees this scripture inside atoms, where it is of no benefit to people, and reflects, "I should make the effort to break open the atoms, one and all, to release this scripture and enable all people everywhere to gain benefit from it." The knowledge of those who arrive at reality is also like this, infinite, pervasive, with the potential to benefit people everywhere.

Then the Realized One observed all living beings in the cosmos with the eye of unobstructed pure knowledge and uttered these words:

How wonderful! How strange! How is it that these beings have the knowledge of those who arrive at reality, yet in ignorance and folly they do not know or see? I should teach them the Way of the wise, to enable them to be free of the fixations of false ideas forever and actually perceive in themselves the vast knowledge of those who arrive at reality, no different from Buddhas.

Then he taught people to practice the noble path to get them to detach from false ideas, and they realized the infinite knowledge of those who arrive at reality, which benefits and comforts all living beings.

The *Comprehensive Scripture of Complete Awareness* says,

All living beings experience complete awareness. When they meet teachers, depending on the principles and practices they make basic, then their practice may be immediate or gradual, but if they find the right route of practicing the unsurpassed enlightenment of those who arrive at reality, then they all attain buddhahood regardless of whether their faculties are great or small.

If you want to master this path, first you need the faculty of great faith. What is the faculty of faith? It means faith in the inherence of the nature of mind and the immeasurable knowledge of all Buddhas; faith that those who cultivate it will realize it, regardless of the magnitude of their potential or the degree of their intelligence; faith that as the power of concentration develops various states will occur and if you mistake them for enlightenment you'll fall into the categories of the two vehicles or outsiders; faith that when the time comes and effort has been sufficient, the enlightened nature will suddenly appear, without making use of intellectual discrimination; faith that even if the enlightened nature suddenly appears, if you don't see a teacher and don't pass through multiple barriers, you will have wasted your life; faith that even if you pass through multiple barriers and attain the essence of Zen, our school's last bit of progressive transcendence has a distinct life; faith that even if you attain that bit of experience beyond, power and function are not equal, depending on individual application, involving a lot of detail; faith that the succession of teachers has a reason, and efforts to continue true Zen should not be neglected; faith that every lifetime from here on is one thing, cultivation of the Way; faith in upholding the experience of progressive transcendence and communicating it to the future, not letting it die out.

When you have developed a resolute mind in this way, you can make great vows, vowing never to give up until you attain penetrating insight into essential nature; vowing to remain sunk forever rather than entertain a single thought of retreat; vowing to go to hell rather than be deluded by popular teachings and rather than accept visionary states and thus fall into the views of the two vehicles or outsiders; vowing to carry out the acts of bodhisattvas forever once insight into essential nature is penetrating; vowing not to give up without understanding each and every one of the verbal teachings of Buddhas and Masters; vowing not to give up without penetrating progressive transcendence; vowing not to give up without equaling the Buddhas and Masters in power and application; vowing not to develop a lowly mentality and disgrace the way of the school; vowing not to be insincere and crave human sentiment; vowing to produce one or two genuine successors to perpetuate the way of the school to thank the Buddhas and Masters, to practice the acts of bodhisattvas lifetime after lifetime, generation to generation, ultimately to liberate all living beings.

When you have made great vows like this, and made the vows of all Buddhas your own vows, made the will and conduct of the Zen masters your own will and conduct, general vows and particular vows may be activated at will. Pray sincerely every day; think about them all the time. Just as the atmosphere sustains the earth, the atmosphere of great vows sustains buddhahood. Just as a favorable wind drives a boat, for the ocean of the essence of reality there is the boat of insight, which cannot move but for the wind of knowledge from great vows. Those of you who tarry along the way in the mentalities of the three vehicles and the views of outsiders, the reason you cannot plumb the profound wellspring of the Buddhas and Masters is that the strength of your vows is inadequate.

The *Combined Treatise on the Flower Ornament* says,[1] "To fulfill the teachings employed by all Buddhas alike with the first inspiration is called riding the vehicle of all knowledge. If compassion, knowledge, vows, and conduct are at all unlike the Buddhas, even faith won't be possible, much less abiding in the abode of Buddhas." It also says, "If one's aspiration is at all unlike the compassion, knowledge, vows, and conduct of the spiritual personality cultivated by those who arrive at reality, one cannot be called a newly inspired bodhisattva." So I ask people who study the path to develop this attitude first.

If you are greathearted, even if you don't work on it, it will still be a field of blessings and ultimately will become an excellent condition for the future. How much the more so if you go on to cultivate and enhance it, mastering the path as best you can.

The correct course for cultivating practice is based on vows. If the strength of your vows is deep and weighty, demons and outsiders cannot disturb you; if the strength of your vows is slight and superficial, you will encounter many obstacles.

Now then, the strength of vows is rooted in compassion. Those who seek their own benefit all remain within a small perspective. They are like merchants: those who plan for their own success take pride in a little wealth first; those who want to be charitable to everyone else never think a little is enough.

For this reason, the practice of the four universal vows first makes liberation of others the number one pledge, along with clarifying your own nature, cutting off the root of afflictions, studying all teachings, and carrying out the activities of

---

1. By Li Tongxuan, a renowned lay Buddhist of Tang-dynasty China. *Entry into the Realm of Reality* contains a translation of the portion of this commentary covering the *Gandvyuha* portion of the *Avatamsaka-sutra*.

bodhisattvas, so compassion and knowledge are completely fulfilled. This is called the way of Buddhas.[2]

You should realize that great compassion is the foundation
for actual attainment of buddhahood. Observe all people thoroughly, how they ignore basics and pursue trivia, greedily fixated
on avaricious occupations, dying here and born there, compulsively repeating all sorts of futile routines. In the heavens there
are five deteriorations;[3] in the human realm there are eight difficulties;[4] the conditions of hungry ghosts, animals, and hells are
extremely painful. Try to compare their states of mind with your
own state of mind.

Furthermore, all living beings are your parents and siblings
over lifetimes and generations, to whom your gratitude and love
ought to be as toward your present parents and siblings. Considering this, you certainly must develop an attitude of great compassion.

The section on the practical vows of Universal Good in the
Flower Ornament Scripture says,

> If you make sentient beings happy, you make all Buddhas
> happy. Why? Because the heart of great compassion is the
> substance of the Buddhas. Therefore they develop great
> compassion on account of sentient beings, develop the will
> for enlightenment based on great compassion, and attain

2. "The four universal vows" are "Living beings are infinite; I vow to liberate
them. Afflictions are endless; I vow to stop them. The teachings are innumerable; I vow to study them. The way of Buddhas is supreme; I vow to fulfill it."

3. The heavens are meditation states; "deteriorations" refers to people coming back down to earth, out of these abstractions. This is described in terms
at once concrete and metaphorical: their clothes get dirty, the flowers of their
crowns wither and fade, their armpits sweat, their bodies stink, and they are
uncomfortable where they are.

4. "The eight difficulties" refers to the difficulty of attaining enlightenment
in eight conditions: hellish states, animalistic states, extreme greediness, a
meditative paradise of apparent perpetuity, an earthly paradise of longevity,
blindness and deafness, intellectual brilliance, and birth before or after the
time of a Buddha.

true awakening on the basis of the will for enlightenment. It is like a giant tree in a desert; if the roots find water, then the branches, leaves, flowers, and fruits all flourish. The giant tree of enlightenment in the desert of birth and death is also like this. All living beings are the root of the tree; the Buddhas and bodhisattvas are the flowers. Benefit living beings with the water of great compassion and you can obtain the flowers and fruits of knowledge and wisdom of Buddhas and bodhisattvas.

So great compassion is like the sky, because it covers all living beings; great compassion is like the earth, because it produces all the teachings; great compassion makes it possible to see buddha-nature, by first clarifying real knowledge for the sake of others. Great compassion makes it possible to pass through unyielding barriers, by plumbing the profound teachings more and more for the sake of others. Great compassion makes it possible to penetrate the transcendental, by seeking a life beyond for others. Great compassion can develop powerful application, by striving on this path for the sake of others. Great compassion can activate intrepidness, by keeping a vigorous will alive for the sake of others. Great compassion makes it possible to get beyond regression, because the mind is settled for the sake of others. Great compassion can produce broad learning, by studying everything for the sake of others. Great compassion can produce erudition, by deep deduction of the principles of things for the sake of others. Great compassion can produce blessings, by always coming up with expedients for others. Great compassion can annihilate afflictions, by sacrificing body, life, and goods for others. Great compassion can extirpate conceit, by acting benevolently for others. Great compassion enables detachment from fame and profit, by basing everything on truth for the sake of others. Great compassion enables entry into the realm of reality, because there is nowhere it does not go for the sake of others.

The virtues of great compassion are infinite; they could be expounded upon forever without exhausting them, but it boils down to this: Whoever has great compassion can extinguish all obstructions caused by past actions and can fulfill all virtues; no principle cannot be understood, no path cannot be practiced, no knowledge not attained, no virtue not developed. Just as when you want to win people's hearts you first love their children, the Buddhas and bodhisattvas consider all living beings their children, so if you love all living beings equally, all the Buddhas will be moved to respond.

Just propitiating the Buddhas only benefits one individual; Buddhas have complete virtue and knowledge, so they never seek offerings of support from others. Now, if you serve them by means of great compassion, the Buddhas will be deeply pleased and the benefits will extend to the entire universe. It's like the difference between addressing an individual and addressing a crowd when teaching the Dharma. The Dharma itself is no more or less, and neither is its efficacy. The effort to enable everyone else to attain enlightenment first actually collects their virtues and makes them into your own vows. The former and the latter assist each other, back and forth endlessly.

And this principle applies even to material charity. If you pick out someone to give things to, you only please one person, whereas if you give to everyone, even those who don't get any themselves will feel sincere gratitude and be psychologically satisfied by virtue. Therefore all your achievements, virtues, and their results and rewards should always be dedicated to supreme enlightenment for all living beings.

You should think in these terms: "May all living beings gain access to the knowledge and vision of Buddhas; may all living beings be cleared of obstructions caused by past actions; may all living beings attain acceptance of truth; may all living beings concentrate intensely on the path; may all living beings actually experience *samadhi*; may all living beings' knowledge and insight be clear; may all living beings master expedients; may all living beings' vows of compassion be universal; may all living beings' spiritual powers be uninhibited; may all living beings be ultimately fulfilled."

Also, according to what you hear or see, always take this attitude: "How sad that all living beings have fallen into the

bottomless pit of birth and death! How can I contrive to res-
cue them quickly and enable them to rest on the ground of all
knowledge?"

The *Scripture Spoken by Vimalakirti* says, "If you yourself are
in bondage, you cannot release others from bondage." So if you
want to liberate all living beings, it is urgent to seek all knowledge. To seek all knowledge, first you must see essential nature.
It is not that you attain buddhahood yourself and then liberate
living beings; it is in order to liberate living beings that you yourself seek to become a Buddha. And it is not to attain buddhahood
yourself that you liberate living beings; it is for the sake of living
beings that you practice the way of Buddhas everywhere.

Therefore students should first give up selfishness and not fixate on their own benefit. The *Nirvana Scripture* says, "Inspiration and consummation are ultimately not different. Of these
two states of mind, the first is more difficult: 'Not having attained salvation myself, I save others first.' Therefore I honor the
initial inspiration." So students should first relinquish selfishness and not be focused on their own benefit. Those who act for
their own sake only profit one individual and haven't the heart
to liberate others, so they don't clarify the infinite doctrines and
they don't save anyone, so they don't amass infinite spiritual
wealth.

This is why disciples and solitary illuminates appear inferior,
to illustrate the meaning of bias and sterility in aspiration and
action, while Buddhas and bodhisattvas provisionally show signs
of greatness and marks of distinction to represent the principle
of completeness of virtue and knowledge. Later people mistakenly thought that the two vehicles and outsiders have different
natures and don't exist in the present; what they don't realize
is that these are different names for students' knowledge and
practice.

If you seek Buddha outside of mind, this is called being an
outsider. If you abandon the way of your own mind and seek the
ways of others and therefore mistakenly stick to various views,
this is called being a devil; when you hear the true teaching,
you will repudiate it. Therefore to first realize the principle of

emptiness on initiation into Buddhas is called discipleship. Everything being reduced to emptiness, when one does not seek any doctrine but awakens on one's own through conditions, not developing compassionate knowledge, this is called conditional or solitary illumination, roaming spontaneously, enjoying the path alone. Thus gradually developing compassionate knowledge, beneficial to both self and others, is called the Vehicle of Bodhisattvas and is also called the Temporary Great Vehicle—though one has realization of enlightenment, one is not yet free and so has fear of the ocean of birth and death. Therefore some like nirvana; some seek the Pure Land. They cannot fully attain power and fearlessness.

Now if you arouse a great, heroic, powerful will, clearly see through buddha-nature, thoroughly examine all the teachings of differentiation within essential nature, so that they are as clear to you as something you see in the palm of your hand; and after that take up progressive transcendence, acquire the claws and fangs of the cave of the Dharma, and with unimpeded freedom liberate everyone, practicing the conduct of bodhisattvas lifetime after lifetime, generation after generation, never ever thinking of retreat, this is called the One Vehicle of Buddhahood. It is also called the True Great Vehicle, and also the Fundamental Vehicle, the Highest Vehicle, and the Vehicle of All Knowledge. This is called ultimate real true liberation; this is called a bodhisattva *mahasattva.*[5] Is this not the work of a stalwart?

If you want to complete the true path, you must be thoroughgoing. Students nowadays call themselves wearers of the patch robe as soon as they enter Zen communities; following others in their activities, they gradually develop aspiration for enlightenment, but they don't yet know the original intent of leaving home, do not study the practices and vows of bodhisattvas, do not look into the conduct of the ancients, do not believe in the multiple barriers of Buddhas and Masters. Covering their eyes with their hands, they blindly expound Zen and explain the Way,

---

5. *Mahasattva* means "great being," a descriptive term for advanced bodhisattvas.

just hoping to open a big mouth some day to belittle others and enjoy life with an exalted reputation. Because of this, work on the Way is not done, and vows are not carried out, but they gradually gain fame and profit, putting on all manner of poses and appearances.

If you are genuine wayfarers, do not emulate this decadent custom. Get to know the strictures and difficulties of the road, the passes and the obstacles, and only then set out. Entering in directly, let go of your preexisting fixations and minimize your entanglements; make your footsteps light and your sense of the Way heavy. Don't seek fame and gain, don't mix in worldly thoughts. Your heart will become joyful, as if you were setting out on the road back home, like you were going into a mine of gold and jade, like you have become an emperor. Keep on this way thought to thought, and you can congeal a mass of wonder.

Right now, what is this? What is it that sees? What is it that hears? What is it that moves? What is it that sits? At all times, in all places, focus on your mind and see how it is. Without conceiving of being or nonbeing, without thinking of affirmation or negation, without discriminating, without rationalizing, just observe in this way. When the time comes it will appear of itself, without need of your intellectual discrimination. As soon as you conceive discrimination, you obscure original essential nature— then even if you labored forever, you couldn't get it.

If thoughts are flying around, consider this story: "Does a dog have buddha-nature? No." Bring it to mind directly, and don't interpret it logically. Don't interpret it as flavorless; don't interpret it as nothing. If you conceive any logical understanding, you'll never complete the work. But don't develop an illogical mind either. Logic and no logic are after all random ideas. Just bring it up and look at it. It has nothing to do with interpretation; it is the real way of practice of the Buddhas. Continue moment to moment, whether speaking or silent, active or quiet, walking, standing, sitting, and lying down—do not forget it! Or if you occasionally forget, don't lose power.

This is like learning archery—it takes a long, long time to hit the bull's-eye. Just develop the will to persevere; be careful not to flag and slack. If you give up this teaching, by what teaching can you attain liberation? And if you are not liberated, you cannot escape vicious cycles. And how do the pains and troubles of vicious circles compare to the toils and pains of Zen study? How does the fun of false thinking compare to the delight of seeing essential nature? Even the temporal glory of a human king is still considered noble; how much more a king of the supreme Dharma!

Once you've developed a great heart and do not regress moment to moment, the achievement becomes perceptible. Those who detach from birth and death but do not clarify the Way are like birds who want to fly without wings, like trees that want to flourish without roots. Please think about this.

Zen Master Dahui said,

> If you do not retreat from your initial inspiration moment to moment, taking your consciousness from its focus on worldly troubles and returning it to insight, then even if you do not break through in this lifetime, still when you're facing death you won't be dragged down by bad habits into bad states. In the next life you'll surely be able to actually experience insight, according to the power of your vows in this life. This is a certain fact, not to be doubted.

How much more if your investigation is unremitting—the great Dharma will become manifest, like pointing to the palm of your hand.

Just let go of gain and loss and affirmation and negation all at once, and examine directly right where you are: when sitting, examine while sitting; when active, examine while active; when lying down, examine while lying down; when eating, examine while eating; when speaking, examine while speaking; when doing all tasks, examine while doing all tasks.

Suppose a precious jewel you had hidden away at home got lost one day and you didn't know where it was. When you search high and low and still can't find it, you're uneasy in mind. Twenty-four hours a day, no matter what you're doing, you surreptitiously keep looking, far and near. Whose business is this? And what is buddha-nature like? Who is the *you* that it is like?

There may be those who, on reading such a discourse on the power of vows, may mistakenly imagine they have no part in it and cannot follow it in practice. What they don't realize is that this is an expedient for developing an initial attitude of faith, an ancient precedent for inspiring the initial outset of practice. It is like a child's first copybook—the letters are not even completely formed, let alone skillful. Mature or not, it's all a matter of long-term practice. One should progress in study as much as possible according to the teacher's method. The same is true of the vows of students of the Way; although incapable at first, eventually they'll succeed. Even if temporarily discouraged by obstruction caused by ingrained habits, if you can keep your vows in mind you will return to your original mind before long.

For this reason, those who are basically lazy ought to rely on these vows all the more; those whose faith is shallow ought to rely on these vows all the more; those who are dull and ignorant ought to rely on these vows all the more. Those whose perception of nature is clear ought to rely on these vows all the more; those whose intellectual functions are independent ought to rely on these vows all the more. From the first inspiration in the beginning to the final consummation in the end, all depends upon the practical power of these vows. Recite them outwardly; keep mindful of them inwardly. Pray earnestly every day; think about them time and again. Their unconscious influence, like fog moistening clothes, like fragrance adhering to things, naturally enables you to attain the degree of consciousness of the Buddhas and Masters, so self-help and helping others are both fulfilled.

[3]

VISIONARY STATES

As the power of concentration gradually matures in people learning the Way, afflictions weaken bit by bit and beautiful experiences occur from time to time. These are called good states. At such times, you may develop a vision of emptiness of phenomena, or a vision of uniform equality, or a vision of completeness, or a vision that this very being is It.[1] Various perceptions occur, according to one's power of concentration.

The *Heroic Progress Scripture* says,

> You individual illuminates and disciples who still have to learn, today turn your minds toward the supreme sublime awakening of great enlightenment. I have now explained the method of authentic cultivation, but you still don't recognize the subtle bedevilments in the practice of cessation and observation. When hallucinations appear to you and you can't recognize them as such, your cleaning of your mind is incorrect and you fall into false views. It may be the bedevilments of your mental and physical constituents or it may be celestial bedevilment or you may become possessed or bewitched. If your mind is not clear, you mistake thieves for your own children.

---

1. Vision does not refer to ocular visions or other sensory phenomena, but to mystical experiences; while rigorously distinguished from enlightenment, such phenomena are also definitively distinguished from *makyo*, hallucinations and delusions produced or potentiated by neurological stress in concentration.

Then again, some attain a little and consider that enough, like the ignorant monk in the fourth meditation who mistakenly claimed to have realized sainthood.[2] When his heavenly rewards came to an end and signs of deterioration began to appear, he repudiated arhats as being subject to further existence, and fell into uninterrupted hell. It also says, "When you don't consider it holy, it's called a good state; if you interpret it as saintly, you'll be subject to a multitude of deceits." It also says, "There are some demons that enter the heart."

That scripture clearly defines fifty kinds of visionary states. How sad that students today mostly mistake visionary states for realization of enlightenment. For this reason devotees of demons are not few—they subsequently sit at a sanctuary, draw in so many good people, and cause them all to fall into false views, without either party knowing. Instead they call it wonderful supreme enlightenment.

Some make a cult of profound stillness in the wellspring of mind; some make a cult of ordinary unconcern; some make a cult of beating and shouting; some make a cult of denying creation and destruction; some make a cult of not establishing any doctrine. Some consider the verbal teachings of Buddhas and Masters to be secondary and discard them all; some force arbitrary subjective interpretation on the verbal teachings of Buddhas and Masters, and expound various theories. Some make an understanding of flavorlessness, or make an understanding of spells, or make an understanding out of caning, or make an understanding out of shouting, or make an understanding of the thieving mentality. People like this are common; all of them mistakenly acknowledge visionary states and construe them as understanding. Eventually they wind

2. "The fourth meditation" is characterized as having four elements: (1) neither pain nor pleasure, also rendered as neutrality of sensation; (2) relinquishment; (3) mindfulness; (4) single-mindedness. Beyond these are four formless states, also called four empty concentrations: (1) absorption in the infinity of space; (2) absorption in the boundlessness of consciousness; (3) absorption in infinite nothingness; (4) absorption in neither perception nor no perception. According to the traditional definition, the Buddhist arhat, or saint, masters these exercises and experiences but is not confined to them or defined by them.

up on the paths of disciples, solitary illuminates, outsiders, or devils, yet without realizing it themselves.

The *Scripture on Complete Awareness* says, "If people seek good friends but instead meet those with false views and do not attain true enlightenment, they are called outsiders. It is the mistake of false teachers, not the fault of the people." How regrettable when people become monks known as teachers and eminent worthies, yet wind up in the category of these phonies! High-minded people who genuinely study mysticism should know this and not be deluded by them, not lapping up the aforementioned fox slobber, not letting charlatans take advantage.

The ninety-six types of outsiders, as well as the most evil devil, think they have attained supreme enlightenment.[3] Therefore wayfarers must first distinguish bedevilments. Any views that differ at all from Buddha are views of outsiders. Just meticulously observe objectively. Don't think it's easy. Even the worst sinners have some hope of deliverance, but there is no getting out of the consequences of false views.

As clearly defined in the letters of Zen Master Dahui, these are states of bedevilment. What are people of later times thinking when they ignore this? It's a result of having no genuine guide. How sad!

Please arouse an attitude of intense determination, and take another step forward. The abode of treasure is near; don't linger in the magical castle.[4]

People of old went to many bitter pains before they accomplished this path—are we to be any exception? We have been born and have died over and over since beginningless time, suffering all sorts of misery, but something must have happened

---

3. In the time of the historical Buddha there were said to be ninety-six other schools of philosophy, of which six were particularly prominent. "The most evil devil" is Mara Papiyan, the Most Evil Destroyer, said to reside in the sixth sense, that is, the cognitive faculty. Mara Papiyan personifies the delinquent intellect, called most evil because of its capacity for creating confusion and delusion, and fostering greed and aggression.

4. "The abode of treasure" represents complete enlightenment; "the magical castle" represents peaceful nirvana.

in the meantime to enable us to have come forth in a context of the teaching of a past Buddha so we hear of the Way; yet because of the depth and gravity of obstruction by ingrained habits, we have been lost until now. Now we are hearing the teaching for the first time and have not mastered it through long practice. It's like suddenly bestowing kingship on a commoner—how could it be easy? Just determine to reach the state realized by Buddhas and Masters, and don't regard a little gain to be sufficient.

In ancient times when Buddha was in the world, there were already attainments of three vehicles. Disciples realized emptiness and took it to be nirvana; they didn't seek the totality of Buddha's teachings at all. Individual illuminates discovered the nature of reality on their own and thought relying on nature and having no concerns was the ultimate end. Bodhisattvas practiced the six perfections together on the path they attained. In this way they each attained resulting realizations and were able to develop spiritual capacities and the powers of the path. But this was not the way of authentic perception of essential nature, so they were criticized in the Universal scriptures.

There are also two different kinds of three vehicles—attained by study and stopped along the way. That is to say, first believing in the teachings of the three vehicles, each individual attains the resulting realization according to capacity; this is referred to as being attained by study. Alternatively, even if your faith is in the One Vehicle, if you stop along the way to indulge in the results and do not progress further, this is called stopping along the way.

For example, suppose you are aiming for the county or prefecture seat; when you arrive, you can reside there. Then again, suppose your aim is the royal capital, but along the way you mistake the county seat or the prefecture seat for the royal capital. Now if you make the crowning Zen of the Buddhas the basis of your study but your faith is insufficient, as a consequence, you stop at a small view.

The three vehicles and five natures are all stages in the process of practicing the path.[5] It is like learning archery. The aim is the target, but those whose strength is inadequate are unsteady of eye and foot, so their arrows don't hit the target, falling far away. Even though there is that subtle wondrous Way, yet the fulfillment of it ultimately is not beyond the results obtained by the three vehicles. Therefore I include great views and small views, all realizations, within the category of visionary states. I only ask that you pay attention and be careful. Even if you have attained genuine perception of essential nature, there are still locks of differentiation, and the road beyond; how much more for those who haven't yet seen nature.

When people of old have spoken of attainment at a single stroke without going through any process, it just means that attainment of buddhahood is basically in an instant—only thus does this make sense. It is like hitting a target; it's up to a single arrow—a follow-up arrow won't help it.

Now because you can't discern the target and you misperceive the target, you create so much debate. So if you want to shoot the target, first distinguish the false from the true. If the target isn't right, it's not real even if you hit it.

Generally, when your mind is simple and straightforward, there are basically no terms such as true or false. When you err to the point of taking the unreal for the real, then there is an issue of right and wrong. This is why koans originated. When you get here, please be lively and do not think you have attained what you have not yet attained or that you have realized what you have not yet realized. Even if you have some very deep realizations, they are all visionary states, not real buddhahood.

Dahui said, "Great enlightenment, eighteen times; little enlightenments, I don't know how many." He already had a great heart, so he was no pushover for bedeviling states. When he first met Yuanwu, he thought to himself, "I'll complete nine summers,

5. Again, "the five natures" refer to the psychologies associated with the three vehicles plus those of indefinite nature and those with no such nature.

and if he approves me like they have everywhere else, I'll write a treatise on the nonexistence of Zen." See how the people of old developed great capacity like this. Nowadays, as soon as people gain a bit of knowledge or half an understanding, they all consider the great matter concluded. As for their teachers and teachings, they exchange stamps of approval, testifying to this as genuine Buddhism.

Even worse are those who, on hearing that talk of mind and nature, take it to be Zen. Boasting of the principle of inherence, they do not believe in the ancients' explanations of true realization. Therefore Zen Master Yuanwu said, "Suppose someone comes out here and says there is originally no transcendence and no accommodation, so why study? I would just tell him, 'I knew you were living in a ghost cave.'" He said, "What a pity! Many people later rationalized that 'crude words and subtle speech all wind up at ultimate truth.' If you understand this way, go be a professor, where you can spend your life profiting from lots of knowledge and lots of interpretation." He also said,

> Now it is often said that there is originally no enlightenment but a teaching of enlightenment is created to construct this task. If you understand this way, you're like parasites on a lion's body, feeding yourselves on the lion's flesh. Have you not seen how an ancient said, "If the source is not deep, the flow does not last. If knowledge is not great, vision is not far-reaching." If you interpret it as a construct, how could Buddhism have reached the present day?[6]

Unfortunately, things were thus even in ancient times—how can we be proud these days? I beg those who have the will not to ignorantly imitate others. Guishan's *Admonitions* says, "I humbly hope you develop a determined, intense will, open up a heart of extraordinary attainment, and in your conduct observe those

---

6. These quotes from Yuanwu are combined excerpts and paraphrases from his commentaries in *The Blue Cliff Record*, cases 77 and 71.

who are superior; don't selfishly follow the mediocre and the inferior. You need resolution in this life; consider that it does not depend on another."[7]

Also, Zen Master Dazhi of Baizhang said, "If you want to know the meaning of buddha-nature, observe timing and conditions. Once the time is ripe, it is like suddenly understanding after having been confused, like suddenly remembering after having forgotten. Then you will have insight into yourself, which is not gotten from another."[8]

Students should just take up the story they are concentrating on energetically, and some day it will naturally become obvious. It's like someone from the countryside who wants to go to the capital city for the first time. As soon as he emerges into central territory, he may see the evenness of the roads or he may see the magnificence of the buildings or he may see the grandeur of the castles, things he's never seen before, and erroneously imagine he's in the capital city. But if he finds a knowledgeable guide who's already been there, he won't stop along the way, but will go right into the capital, paying no attention to the administrative halls or the imperial chambers, only really aiming to meet the ruler in person.

7. See "The House of Kuei-Yang" in *The Five Houses of Zen* for further excerpts from this work.

8. See *The Five Houses of Zen* on "Pai Chang" in "The House of Kuei-Yang"; see also *The Pocket Zen Reader*, pp. 35–52, 175, 219; *Teachings of Zen*, pp. 14–19; *The Blue Cliff Record*, cases 26, 70–72; *Book of Serenity*, case 8; and *Unlocking the Zen Koan*, case 2.

[4]

TRUE REALIZATION

In lofty-minded people who genuinely work on the path, when the effort of inner seeking builds up and the power of concentration is full, then ordinary ideation and conscious feelings are all inactivated; reason and speech come to an end, and even the searching mind disappears at the same time. Even the breath nearly stops. This is the time when the Great Way appears.

Students should be alert: At this time, don't conceive a single thought of extraordinary understanding, and don't conceive a single thought of retreating. Let go of body and mind and don't seek anything at all. Bring the story you've been contemplating powerfully to mind, and let whatever states may appear be: if the perceptions of the two vehicles appear, let them be; if the perceptions of outsiders appear, let them be—knowing they aren't real, you won't fear them. Plunging in with your whole body, get your fill of the source, carefully avoiding exciting your mind to grasp and reject.

You need to let go of your body and relinquish your life therein only once. When the time comes, it happens suddenly, and you know this experience. This is called letting go of your grip over a sheer cliff, then after perishing, coming back to life. Suddenly, in an instant, you recognize the root source: your own nature, the nature of others, the nature of living beings, the nature of afflictions, the nature of enlightenment, the nature of Buddhas, the nature of spirits, the nature of bodhisattvas, the nature of the created, the nature of the uncreated, the nature of the ultimate end, the nature of the sentient, the nature of the insentient, the nature of ghosts, the nature of titans, the nature of beasts, hells, heavens, polluted lands, and pure lands—you see through them all at once, without exception, finishing the great task and passing through birth and death. How could it not be pleasant?

Even so, in order to test what you've experienced, call on a great Zen teacher who is definitely certain. An ancient said, "The heart of nirvana is easy to clarify; knowledge of differentiation is hard to illumine." Don't let undifferentiated knowledge obscure knowledge of differentiation.

It is like polishing a mirror: The moment its clear surface is exposed, it can distinguish all things. The coarse appears coarse, the fine appears fine; blue, yellow, red, white, pretty, ugly, big, small, square, round, long, short—they are reflected as they appear, without so much as a particle or tip of a hair left out.

When this occurs, if there is anything unclear, this just means that even though the clarity is there, residual defilement has not yet been removed; the traces of polishing are still there, blocking the reality. This is why we don't conceive the notion we have already attained, and don't think of stopping, but seek certainty with an enlightened teacher in order to test our attainment.

In ancient times, when Sushan first heard Xiangyan say, "The issue of speech is not sound; before form, there is no thing," he experienced a liberating enlightenment and thought he had thoroughly comprehended. He promised, "When you have a place to live, mentor and elder brother, I will come see to firewood and water." Later he also heard Zen Master Da-an of Guishan's saying, "Propositions of being and nothingness are like vines clinging to a tree," and went to Guishan especially for this, having "sold off a place mat a thousand miles away," also thinking he was right.

Guishan was plastering a wall when Sushan asked, "'Propositions of being and nothingness are like vines clinging to a tree'—is this your saying?"

Da-an said, "Yes."

Sushan said, "Suppose the tree falls down and the vines die—where do the propositions wind up?"

Da-an put down the plaster trowel, laughed out loud, and went back to his room.

Sushan said, "I sold off a place mat a thousand miles away to come here just for this—why don't you explain for me?"

Da-an called to an attendant, "Fetch some cash and give it to this midget *acarya*," and said to Sushan, "Someday there will be a one-eyed dragon who will point it out for you."

Later Sushan went to Mingzhao and brought up the preceding story. Mingzhao said, "Guishan was correct start to finish, but he didn't meet a connoisseur."

Sushan said, "If the tree falls and the vines die, where do the propositions wind up?"

Mingzhao said, "You're renewing Guishan's laughter."

Sushan was greatly enlightened at these words. He said, "Guishan had a sword in his laugh all along," and bowed to him at a distance to repent of his error.

Then when Xiangyan appeared in the world, Sushan kept his earlier promise and went to call on him.

When Xiangyan went up in the teaching hall, a monk asked, "How is it when one does not seek the sages and does not esteem one's own spirit?"

Xiangyan said, "Myriad impulses cease, the thousand sages do not accompany."

Sushan, hearing this, made a sound as of vomiting.[1]

See how he first thought Xiangyan was somebody, but then when he knew the business of the Zen school, on hearing Xiangyan's statement he was like an aristocrat hearing a field hand talk. This is why students should first visit an enlightened teacher as soon as they attain perception of essential nature, to get rid of confusion within enlightenment.

In olden times, Huanglong Sixin said, "When you have confusion, you need to attain enlightenment. Once you have attained enlightenment, you need to recognize confusion within enlightenment, and enlightenment within confusion."[2] You should realize that this is a good time to seek an enlightened

1. See *Book of Serenity*, case 87, for classical commentaries on this story.
2. For more from this master, one of the early luminaries of the Huanglong sect, see *The Pocket Zen Reader*, pp. 63, 72; and *Zen Lessons*, cases 127–33.

teacher, an experience that tells you now you should cultivate practice. Master Baiyun said, "This matter requires enlightenment to attain it; after enlightenment, it is necessary to meet someone."

You say, "Once enlightened, you're at rest—why do you necessarily need to meet someone?" Those who have met someone after enlightenment will clearly have their own way of expression when it comes to expedient means of reaching out, and will not blind students. Those who have realized a dry turnip will not only blind their students, they themselves will tend to wound their hands on the point. It's no wonder that teachers everywhere today mistakenly blind the eyes of students. Even though you need to see someone, don't see anyone who is not a great Zen master with genuine certainty; otherwise you'll get deluded, hindering your enlightenment.

When I was first traveling, I met several Zen masters whose teaching I wouldn't say was entirely incorrect, but when compared to the likes of Yantou, Xuefeng, Dahui, and Xutang, there were discrepancies.[3] So I always harbored doubt in my heart and did not completely trust them. I thought that Buddhism was already extinct in the present time and no one had accurate knowledge and accurate perception. I thought it would be better to go into the mountains alone and study and practice intensely as the ancients did, waiting for the time by myself.

Later, when I heard of the Way of my former teacher [Hakuin], I half believed and half doubted. I told myself that I couldn't rely on what other people said but should hear him teach before I decide. Then when I received his instruction, it actually accorded with so much of what the ancestral teachers have said through-

3. For Yantou (827–87), see Teachings of Zen, p. 32; The Blue Cliff Record, cases 51 and 66, and the biographical supplement on p. 618; Book of Serenity, case 22; Unlocking the Zen Koan, case 13. For Xuefeng (822–908), see "Hsueh-feng" in "The House of Yun-men" in The Five Houses of Zen; The Blue Cliff Record, cases 5, 22, 49, 51, and the biographical supplement on p. 570; Book of Serenity, cases 24, 34, 50, 55; Unlocking the Zen Koan, case 13. For Dahui, see Swampland Flowers; Zen Lessons, cases 145–51; "Zen Master Dahui" in Zen Essence. For Xutang, see Unlocking the Zen Koan, case 20.

out the ages that my heart was filled with joy. From that point on I gave my life to seeking certainty, to this very day.

In the present time, teachers all over misguide and blind students, because their attainments have not reached the realm personally realized by the ancients. As for the transcendental, when have they ever dreamed of it? Even though it is not that there are originally two or three Buddhisms, there are shallow and deep, crude and fine. It's just because students don't have enough power of faith, they haven't eliminated cognition of states, and they have not extirpated residual habits, that brings about so many distinctions in Buddhism. If even the ancients were like this, how could people now not be so?

A long time ago Master Dongshan provisionally defined five ranks to indicate the essentials of the school.[4] The rank of the absolute is emptiness. The rank of the relative is the temporal. This is not teaching the Tendai contemplation of truths.[5] In that contemplation of truths, first you contemplate the truth of emptiness to break your hold on the idea of existence. Next you contemplate temporal truth to eliminate the sense of lingering in emptiness. When the barriers of being and nothingness are gone, views of emptiness and temporal existence are both forgotten and real essence appears—this is called the truth of the real characteristics of the middle way.

This is a remedial method opposing subject and object. Based on the substance and function of real nature, while provisionally using them to define the terms, one gradually gets to know a part of the principle in nature by means of the power of contemplation. Therefore it is only on reaching the truth of the middle

---

4. Master Dongshan was Liangjie (806–69). See *The Blue Cliff Record,* case 43; *Book of Serenity,* cases 49, 89, 94, 98. The Rinzai treatment of the five ranks device is different from Dongshan's, based on the revision of Fenyang. For more on the original structure, see "Caoshan on the Five Ranks" in *Timeless Spring;* "The House of Ts'ao-Tung" in *The Five Houses of Zen;* and "The Five States of Lord and Vassal," the appendix on traditional teaching devices in *The Blue Cliff Record.* For Hakuin's treatment, see "The Five Ranks" in *Kensho: The Heart of Zen.*

5. On this Tendai method of contemplation, see *Stopping and Seeing,* pp. 113–22.

way that one first sees nature with three contemplations in one mind.[6]

So this teaching of five ranks has been set up to enable those who have seen nature to investigate the deep meanings successively, so as to develop the capacity of great Dharma kings with great vision. How could it be a commonplace doctrine?

What are referred to here as empty and temporal are different names for real nature. The basic substance of real nature is empty and pure; there is nothing to it to name, but the label of emptiness is imposed on it. There is nothing that does not appear in the substance of inherent nature, according to differentiations; the label of temporal is imposed on this.

"The relative within absolute," or "relative absolute," means that even when you see nature accurately, though your insight into yourself is penetrating, your degree of power is weak, and so you are still not completely clear about differentiations. It is like the mirror having some dust left on it, so objects are not thoroughly clear in detail. It is also like reading by moonlight; it's not quite clear what the ideograms are. Therefore the verse says,

The relative within the absolute:
At midnight, before the moon shines,
Don't wonder at meeting without recognition;
Aversion of the past is still hidden in the heart.

This means that even if you see real nature, when it is not yet completely clear you ultimately don't get out of the domain of past ignorance. For this reason the rank of absolute within the relative, or relative absolute, was defined to clarify this point.

If you want to enter absorption in this absolute within the relative, you must study the stories that are hard to penetrate. "The absolute within the relative" means that seeing nature is perfectly clear, without any defilement, and the subtle pat-

---

6. "Three contemplations in one mind" means seeing temporal reality, emptiness, and the middle way all at once. This is a practice of the Tendai school. See *Stopping and Seeing*, p. 34.

terns of differentiation appear in everything. As differentiation becomes clear, the fundamental becomes even clearer; and as the fundamental is clarified, differentiation becomes as clear as can be. When both are perfectly clear, and as a result there is no reflection between them, this is called the absolute within the relative. The verse says,

> The absolute within the relative:
> A woman who got up late is at the antique mirror—
> Clearly she sees her face, but there's no more reality;
> She doesn't mistake the reflection for her head
>   anymore.

Students have been immersed in false views so long that when they first see real nature, differentiations are still not clear for that reason. It's like a woman who woke up late now facing an antique mirror: You clearly see everything, this and that as clear as can be, and yet there are no images—noumenon and phenomena are completely merged, nature and characteristics are not separated. This is said to have no reality, just as when you see your face in the mirror all your features show, so you mistake the image in the mirror for your own head. Whoever acknowledges the mirror of cognition then misses the fundamental substance. But this doesn't refer to the mirror of the other kinds of knowledge; once you see nature with perfect clarity, all knowledge and unhindered intelligence appear. This is the mirror of knowledge.

Therefore, if the function of intelligence is not clear, the fundamental has not been penetrated; when the function of intelligence is clear, you inevitably get stuck in the mirror of cognition. When you get here, you need to seek a different way out. And don't make the mistake of saying that not acknowledging anything at all is right; even if you actually get to the point where you don't acknowledge anything, the garden of Zen is still beyond the horizon. You must be intensely conscious of your everyday experience in the noumenon of seeing nature, inwardly feeling for some reason. Don't think it's easy—the rank of coming from within the absolute is our school's final transcendent way out. So it is said, "Within nothingness is a road out of the dust." "Within nothingness" means when all is complete and everything is done and you seek to advance your practice, after all, nothing is attained. This is called the point where the road ends. You have to go through it too and have a life beyond, for your previous attainment is still not out of the dust. It is only when you reach this road that you get out of the dust. Therefore it is totally impossible to discuss what comes after this—finding the road out to a life beyond is just to be investigated and determined on your own.

Old Master Dongshan provisionally defined terms and made so many explanations only to have you know there is layer after layer of deep meaning; this is not even Dongshan's fundamental intent, so why add rationalizations to increase others' worries? On the whole, it's really hard to find even one or two individuals who successfully pass through "coming from within the absolute," so now in further defining the ranks of *arrival in both* and *attainment in both,* it is really possible to see the unique state of Great Master Dongshan. Xuedou's eulogy says, "His outreach was after all like a myriad-fathom cliff."[7] He can be said to know what he's talking about.

All the Zen teachers past and present who made analyses of this failed to entirely understand this elder's application, so they all miss the meaning of repetition. A pity! This definition of so many ranks to indicate the essentials of the school may seem inferior to Linji and Deshan, but when it comes to leading into the essential meaning, how could there be any superiority or inferiority? He actually circulated this summary secretly, to await powerful descendants, because he feared that in later generations there would be no one who personally mastered the teaching, so the true pulse would be lost.

If students first exert all their strength on coming from within the absolute, someday they'll have a life beyond; then come back and look at the rank of arrival in both to see why it was set up. The verse says,

> Two blades cross points, no need to withdraw
> an expert is like a lotus in fire.

That is to say, this is not the realm of anyone else but experts who have themselves attained the marvel. Therefore you must first reach that realm.

Now what is the principle of the rank of attainment in both? See how the ancient reached out with expedients so that you wouldn't linger in the single principle of seeing nature. In scripture, Manjusri represents the great knowledge of seeing nature, while Samantabhadra represents cultivation of practice after enlightenment.[8] Li Tongxuan says that even if you have Manjusri's great knowledge of seeing nature, without Samantabhadra's refined practice after enlightenment you ultimately fall into the views of the two vehicles.[9]

It is like the teaching of the *Flower Ornament*, where true awakening is attained at the moment of initial inspiration, yet fifty kinds of teachings are subsequently practiced. When Sudhana was at the youth Manjusri's place, he realized initially by faith.[10] Then when he met the monk Meghasri from the peak of the mountain of marvel on a separate peak, the totality appeared completely, and he attained the teaching of the light of knowledge seeing everywhere contemplating the realms of all Buddhas. From here he gradually traveled south, through one hundred and ten cities, calling on fifty-three teachers. Then, based on Maitreya's instruction, he wanted to see Manjusri again.

8. For Manjusri, see *The Flower Ornament Scripture*, books 9–12; for Samantabhadra (Universal Good), see books 36–38. See also book 39, pp. 1159, 1169, 1229, 1502, 1503.

9. See *Entry into the Realm of Reality* for Li's commentary on the final book of the *Flower Ornament Scripture*, which features both figures.

10. The story of Sudhana's pilgrimage is the subject of the final book of the *Flower Ornament*.

Now Manjusri reached out with his right hand, past one hundred and ten leagues, and patted Sudhana on the head. He said, "Good, good! Good man, without the faculty of faith, the mind is weak, anxious, and regretful. If worthy action is insufficient and you shirk diligent effort, dwelling on a single root of good and thinking a little virtue enough, then you cannot skillfully carry out vows and will not be accepted and protected by good friends. You will not be able to comprehend a truth like this, a principle like this, a teaching like this, a practice like this, a realm like this. Whether in respect to comprehensive knowledge or diverse knowledge, you will be unable to plumb the source or understand completely, or enter in, or know how to explain, or analyze, or realize, or attain."

When Manjusri pointed this out to Sudhana, as he spoke Sudhana realized countless truths, was imbued with the immeasurable light of great knowledge, entered into the door of Universal Good, and in a single thought saw as many teachers as atoms in a billion worlds, attended them all, respectfully accepted their assignments, and received and carried out their instructions, attaining liberation of the treasury of adornments of knowledge from mindfulness without forgetfulness.

The scripture goes on to say that Sudhana entered a field in a pore of Universal Good, and in taking a single step in the pore crossed as many worlds as atoms in unspeakably, inexplicably many buddha fields, all with equivalent Samantabhadras, Buddhas, fields, practices, and liberations, all entirely the same, equal, none other, none different.

The *Combined Treatise* says,[11]

> Fifty ways of transcendence in five ranks, five levels of refinement, distinguish breadth and narrowness of knowledge and compassion, rawness and ripeness, liberation and bondage, opposition and accord, combining the different amounts and degrees of virtue and wisdom, to induce aspi-

11. This refers to Li Tongxuan's commentary on the *Flower Ornament Scripture*.

rants not to consider it sufficient to dwell on one teaching, or even three, four, or five, or ten, a hundred, or a thousand. The purpose is to get them to progress and ascend until they reach the infinitely vast realm of reality as is. That is why five ranks are defined therein.

See how the Buddha so kindly and clearly discussed the ranks of the Way for you. All of these are models of progress in real cultivation after enlightenment, expedients where there are no expedients, grades in the gradeless. This is also true of Dongshan's five ranks and Linji's four points of view and four guest-host relations—all of these are models for after enlightenment.[12] Students in the present time do not use expedients like these to test their attainment, rejecting them with the cliché, "What donkey-tethering stakes are these?" That does seem so, but still their views have so much dust and sand. Therefore students should not stop at the one principle of seeing nature and leave off there.

12. "Linji's four points of view" are taking away the subject but not objects, taking away objects but not the subject, taking away both subject and objects, and taking away neither subject nor objects. In the terms of practice used in this treatise, the host stands for seeing nature, and the guest for knowledge of differentiation; the "four guest-host relations" of host and guest are as follows: the guest looks at the host, the host looks at the guest, the guest within the guest, and the host within the host.

[5]

PASSING THROUGH BARRIERS

Great Master Yunmen said, "On level ground the dead are count-less; those who can get out of a forest of thorns are the experts." This is one of the ancients' sayings that are hard to penetrate. The present time is totally degenerate; this is referred to as the dead on flat ground. This is why it's hard to find a genuine Zen teacher.

The *Emerging Sun Scripture* says, "The wise use insight to refine their minds; like iron in ore, it takes hundreds of smelt-ings to produce pure metal, just as it takes constant lapping of the ocean to produce its treasures."

For this reason, Shoju Rojin said,

Zen monks of recent times who take up the saying that a dog has no buddha-nature and approach it authentically with unalloyed effort all pass through, but as soon as they pass through a little, they think they've attained and think they're enlightened. They talk big, but this is just a major sign of bondage, promoting subjective views and increasing egoism. The garden of the ancestors is still far off on the ho-rizon. If you want to reach genuine comfort, the more you understand the more you bring up, the more you compre-hend the more you contemplate, until you actually see the final issue of the Buddhas and Masters as plainly as looking into the palm of your hand.

I ask students to focus your eyes and look—what season is it now? Time is precious. In order to test the teachings you've attained, I've brought up a number of Buddhist scriptures and treatises. Examine carefully and see whether or not what you have attained accords with the scriptures and treatises. If it is disparate or contrary to the scriptures and treatises, your view is biased and also shallow and simplistic.

Speaking from the perspective of seeing nature, how could there be any reason for not being in accord? Those who can understand thoroughly and develop complete knowledge see each and every one of the infinite teachings of the Buddhas with distinct clarity, recognize each and every one of the infinite expedients of the Buddhas with distinct clarity, clearly comprehend every single insight, every single spiritual capacity, every single liberation, every single state, and all the principles of infinite differentiations. The Three Treatises, Characteristics of Phenomena, *Lotus of the Law*, *Ultimate Demise*, *Flower Ornament*, Introductory, Extended, *Transcendent Insight*, and *Esoteric Ornament* merge unhindered, and you see through them all.[1] You do not interpret meanings literally; you do not distort the text by the meaning. You do not confuse multiple teachings with one teaching, and you do not contradict one teaching with multiple teachings. Just understand by natural insight, don't try to figure them out consciously. If you can understand with perfect clarity when you get here, I'll grant that you have the eye to read scripture.

1. These refer to schools, scriptures, and bodies of Buddhist teachings. The Three Treatise school deals with analytic understanding of the emptiness of phenomena. The Characteristics of Phenomena school is based on the doctrine of *only representation*, referring to the descriptive nature of conventional reality as we cognize it. The *Lotus of the Law Scripture* downgrades nirvana to a strategic expedient and introduces visions of One Vehicle and comprehensive enlightenment. The *Scripture of the Ultimate Demise* emphasizes the eternity of the reality underlying the teaching and identifies the Buddha, the Teaching, and the Community with being-as-is. The *Flower Ornament* teaches universal relativity, summarized by the principle "All in one, one in all." The Introductory doctrines refer to the scriptures of the Lesser Vehicle, emphasizing purification and nirvana. The Extended, or Universal, scriptures wean the mind from the Lesser Vehicle to focus on the Great Vehicle. The *Transcendent Insight* scriptures clear the mind of attachment to the teachings as mental objects. *The Esoteric Ornament Scripture* presents the mystic doctrine of buddhahood in this body.

It's like the four characteristics in the *Scripture of Complete Awareness:* These point out dust and sand in views. It says, "States of mind all the way up to realization of the ultimate end of the enlightened and perfect knowledge of pure nirvana are all characteristics of self." It also says, "States of mind all the way up to complete realization of nirvana are all self, because the mind keeps some understanding. If you thoroughly exhaust the principles realized, all are called characteristics of personality." It also says,

All people's realizations and understandings are self and personality. And where the characteristics of self and personality do not reach, keeping possession of objects of understanding is called the characteristic of a sentient being. And what is the characteristic of a life? It means when sentient beings' minds focus on purity and they have a sense of comprehending something, which all conditioned knowledge cannot see, it is like the root of life. If the mind perceives any awareness, it is all considered sense-data pollution, because what awareness is aware of is not apart from sense data.

This is clearly pointed out in the scripture, but how do you apply it? When your insight is clear, this is the very substance of the appearance of self. Knowing that insight is self and relinquishing it is called the appearance of person. Where self and person do not reach is called the appearance of a being. When all appearances vanish and you transcend everything, you still do not escape life. This is called the final bond. Where do Zen monks settle their bodies and establish their lives?

In the present time, people often think that having no intellectual knowledge is Zen, and so they don't use scriptures or treatises. Instead they say, "What is the need for scriptures and treatises in the special transmission outside doctrine?" They still don't realize that when what is outside doctrine is clear, what is in the doctrines doesn't interfere; but if what is outside doctrine does not admit what is in the doctrines, then what is outside doctrine isn't true either. Why? Because when a mirror is clear, it doesn't select what to reflect; if reflections don't appear, it means the mirror isn't clear. You are rejecting the images of objects because of the dust covering the mirror.

If you are on the Great Way, you don't conceive this opinion, especially since there are very deep meanings in the scriptures that can point out so many of your barriers of perception. It is only because your vision is not clear that you repudiate the golden words of the Buddha and cannot find out the hidden meanings in the scriptures that are hard to unlock.

It's not a matter of making a religion of scriptures and treatises, just of using scriptures and treatises as revealing mirrors, using the teaching to reflect our own nature and using our own nature to reflect the teachings. Both must be clearly comprehended.

Scripture also says,

People of the final age who do not comprehend the four appearances may practice the path with diligent intensity for aeons,[2] but this can only be called contrivance—in the end they cannot attain all the realizations of sages. This is the reason it is called the final age of the true teaching. Why? Because the universal self is taken to be nirvana, and having realization and having enlightenment is called fulfillment.

This is quite a lock—don't misunderstand this passage and think it's right to have no realization and no enlightenment. This scripture is based on realization of pure complete awareness. Therefore it says, "If people of the final age hope to complete the Way, don't let them seek enlightenment, as it will only increase their formal learning and magnify their opinion of themselves."

Subsequently it also uses four illnesses to illustrate sicknesses in perception, called construction, cessation, spontaneity, and extinction. The use of knowledge with a sense of understand-

2. "The four appearances" refer to the aforementioned appearances of self, person, being, and life.

ing something is called the illness of construction. Going along with the nature of things, being spontaneous whatever happens, is called the illness of spontaneity. Stopping all perceptions so not a single thought arises is called the illness of cessation. Total annihilation and utter quietude without activity is called the illness of extinction.

Now tell me, how do you apply this in practice? Guifeng mistakenly made this interpretation:[3] "Now the reason they are considered illnesses is because all four lack observing insight." Wrong! Isn't observing insight the substance of the illness of construction? He also says,

> Just because they induce the mind to dwell one-sidedly on one practice, failing to find out the whole meaning from good friends, and in their craving for simplicity hold to one and consider that completeness, this is why the scripture denounces them all as illnesses. If you can master them all, without fixation on one, then you can enter the Way through all four.

Wrong, wrong! If you understand this way, what is the advantage? Even if you can comprehend all four principles and the complete meaning is distinctly clear, when you get here it's like putting thorns in your eyes.

Scriptures such as these have been thoroughly annotated by followers of schools of intellectual interpretation who have all missed Buddha's deep meaning. Zhenjing's discourse on everyone realizing criticizes the raw; Heshan repudiates subjective explanation to warn students.[4] So if you want to read the ancient teachings, don't use annotations. Annotations often obliterate the intent of the original text.

3. Guifeng Zongmi was a scholarly Zen master of Tang-dynasty China; much of his work is lost.

4. Zhenjing was one of the great masters of the Huanglong sect of Zen in Song-dynasty China; see *Zen Lessons*, cases 51–56; *Teachings of Zen*, pp. 67–71. For Heshan, see *The Blue Cliff Record*, case 44.

This means that the mystic messages in the scriptures that are hard to understand go hand in hand with the aforementioned four appearances, like a poison drum, like a bonfire, like a diamond, like lion milk. If students want to understand the deep meanings mentioned and get rid of the afflictions of views mentioned, first of all don't construct random interpretations; just contemplate the sayings that are hard to penetrate. One is this: "The cattle of Huai Province eat grain; the horses of Yi Province get full."

Another is this: "Holding a hoe with empty hands, riding a buffalo while walking on foot, someone crosses a bridge—the bridge flows, not the water." What is the logic of this?

A monk asked Zhaozhou, "Myriad things return to one; where does the one return?" Zhaozhou said, "When I was in Qing Province, I made a cloth shirt that weighed seven pounds."[5]

Yunmen said, "Medicine and disease quell each other. The whole earth is medicine—what is oneself?"[6]

Wuzu said, "It is like an ox going through a window lattice—its head, horns, and four feet have all gone through; why can't the tail get through?"[7]

Sushan's memorial tower incident, Zhaozhou's example of checking out the woman, Jianfeng's three kinds of sickness, Huangbo's dreg slurpers—there are quite a few such koans;[8] just take them up according to your psychological affinities and see what they're about.

This type are all hard to believe, hard to understand, hard to penetrate, hard to enter into. They cannot be seen through easily; like a bonfire, if you get too close they'll burn your face. They are like a sharp sword—mime with it and you lose your life. Just bring them to mind, don't misunderstand. These are not objects

---

5. *The Blue Cliff Record*, case 45.

6. *The Blue Cliff Record*, case 87.

7. *Unlocking the Zen Koan*, case 38.

8. For Zhaozhou, see *Unlocking the Zen Koan*, case 31; *Book of Serenity*, case 10. For Jianfeng, see *Book of Serenity*, commentary to case 46. For Huangbo see *The Blue Cliff Record*, case 11.

of logical understanding or objects of discrimination. They are far beyond ordinary sense, conveying signs in a distinct way.

When students make use of their power to gradually progress along the road, none of them fail to find quite a few signs; then all at once they misuse their minds and think they have fully plumbed the source. Some rejoice, some rest, some open big mouths to explain for others, still unaware that they are just borrowing the power of the sayings to dress up and dignify their own views and this is not the real meaning.

Just keep progressing, and do not stop halfway along. An ancient said, "Those who have attained have mold growing on their mouths." Please keep your mouth shut for now and understand inwardly. Buddhism is not such and such a principle.

In the present time there is also a type who tends to conceive easy views of the koans of the ancients. All alike they look at them and say, "An iron bar has no flavor—ah, ha, ha!" They're like blind men asking about the color of milk: when told it's like a conch, they interpret in terms of sound; told it's like snow, they interpret in terms of cold. Now an "iron bar" does not mean there is no flavor; it means there's nothing you can get your teeth into—this is what's called an iron bar. Just arouse an intense attitude of great fortitude where there is nothing to get your teeth into and chew vertically, chew horizontally, chew and chew unceasingly, and suddenly you'll chew through.[9] Once you've chewed through, you'll find the inexhaustible flavor of Dharma in there. This is called an iron bar—later people didn't understand and misinterpreted it to mean flavorless.

It is like the *Flower Ornament's* great scripture in an atom— you cannot get it without breaking down the atom. So too is the iron bar—if you try to seek Buddhism without chewing through it, you'll never succeed.

Zen Master Wuzu said, "When I arrived at the school of Baiyun,

---

9. Here, "vertically" refers to work in stillness, where intensity and timelessness resemble vertical ascent to the heights as well as vertical descent to the depths, while "horizontally" refers to work in activity, where passing through time and expansive awareness resemble horizontal extent.

I gnawed through an iron beam and found all the hundred flavors contained in it." If an iron bar is not chewed through, then it has no flavor at all, so it might be called flavorless, but if you leave off without savoring it, when can you escape birth and death? It would be like holding the scripture in an atom without extracting it, being falsely acclaimed a reverend, and spending your whole life idle. Even if you labored for eternity, what benefit would there be?

Some say that the *evocation of principle* and *functions* are one, that evocation of principle openly explains principles, while functions covertly indicate principles.[10] This is simply a deceptive idea, making the same mistake as the aforementioned notion of "flavorlessness." Why? The realm perceived when you see essential nature is called attainment of principle. If you just stay in the solitary principle of seeing nature, it sticks to your skin, glued to your bones, and you cannot thoroughly realize the Buddhas' and Masters' subtleties of differentiation. Now in order to remedy this, many differentiating sayings are cited to break through it. These are called functions.

For this reason, Wuzu said, "If you talk about mind and talk about nature, this is foul mouth." Some say that before Mazu and Shitou, everyone taught clearly with principles, while after Mazu and Shitou, from Linji and Deshan on down, they started employing functions, which were not the mystery of the Buddhas and Patriarchs of antiquity. What they do not realize is that the abundant use of principles by the Buddhas and Patriarchs of antiquity was after all indication of the road, not really the inner meaning of the Buddhas and Patriarchs.

You tell me—don't the canonical scriptures adduce principles? Why would the Zen school insist on a source outside doctrine, citing the smile at the flower raised? Why didn't Buddha entrust Kasyapa with principles?[11]

---

10. "Evocation of principle" and "functions" are the first two of three categories of koans in the system of Daio and the first two of five categories of koans in the system of Hakuin's school that Torei and other masters helped to develop.

11. See *Unlocking the Zen Koan*, case 6.

It was just because the people of antiquity were simple and straightforward, innocent and earnest, that when the road was pointed out they proceeded directly to the mystic pass. It's like an intelligent person who heads right home as soon as he finds out the road, whereas the ignorant one will stop somewhere along the way, imagining it's his hometown. When it comes to setting aside the road and pointing directly to the source, Buddha and Masters have all employed functions such as "holding up a flower" and "smiling," and "taking down the flagpole."[12] Now tell me, when you get here, what principle is there to speak of? Can you call these principles? The successors after this just transmitted one experience; their verses on transmission of the Dharma are examples of functions. Is there any such talk in the canon of scriptures? It is like a bonfire, like a diamond sword—if you stand there trying to have a discussion, you'll lose your life.

If you interpret meaning literally, this is of course ordinary talk. How could reverends initiated in the Dharma not know this much? Then what is the meaning individually transmitted one to one in an undeviating lineage? And why did they only receive this Dharma after having already understood mind and attained the Way and then, at last encountering master teachers with the undistorted transmission, following them for many years?

Zen Master Yuanwu said,

Ever since there were masters, they only worked at sole transmission of direct pointing, not liking to drip water and trail mud, set out signs and lay out clichés to make fools of people. Sakyamuni Buddha, at over three hundred assemblies, set up teachings in response to potentials, giving out guidance for the age. It was all very roundabout, so in the end he got down to the essentials to deal with the highest potential. Although the twenty-eight generations from Kasyapa showed some functions, most revealed principle; but when it came time to hand on the transmission, all

---

12. See *Transmission of Light*, case 3; and *Unlocking the Zen Koan*, cases 6 and 22.

without exception presented it directly, like saying "Take down the sanctuary flagpole," putting a needle on a bowl of water, showing a circle, taking hold of a red banner, picking up a clear mirror. They uttered verses transmitting the Dharma that were like iron bars.

Bodhidharma refuted six sects and proved his doctrine to outsiders, so the world was at peace.[13] He spun "I am a deity, you're a dog,"[14] his spiritual workings so swift they could not be figured out by discussion or thought. Then when he came to Liang and traveled to Wei, he openly spoke of the purely transmitted mind-seal outside of doctrine.[15] The instructions of the six generations of grand masters were explicit and obvious. When it came to the Great Mirror of Caoqi, he showed mastery of explanation and mastery of the source in detail.[16]

After the passage of a long time, greatly liberated Zen masters with accurate perception changed in order to clear the way, so that long lingering over names and forms would not fall into abstract discussion. They released lively, free, independent, subtle functions. Eventually we see the use of caning and shouting, dismissing words by means of words, taking away devices by means of devices, attacking poison with poison, refuting actions with actions.

See how that man of old explained thoroughly with distinct clarity. The fact is that since the Middle Ages, people's character has been perverted and twisted, so they linger over the process, greedy to realize the results. Therefore locked gates were provi-

---

13. See J. C. Cleary, *Zen Dawn*, for work attributed to Bodhidharma.

14. This refers back to Kanadeva, the successor of the Nagarjuna, who is associated with the exposition of emptiness and the middle way. The Chinese Three Treatise school of Buddhism is based on the works of Kanadeva and Nagarjuna. For this dialogue, see *The Blue Cliff Record*, commentary to case 13.

15. This refers to the transplantation of Zen to China by Bodhidharma. See *The Blue Cliff Record*, case 1.

16. For the teachings attributed to this master, Huineng, see *The Sutra of Huineng: Grand Master of Zen*.

sionally set up to ascertain what had been attained. These are called *koans,* "official decisions." This is like officials at a pass checking for authenticity before allowing entry. If you want to go to the capital city without passing through the checkpoints, you'll never find a way. If you manage to get through each checkpoint of functions, the principles explained by the Buddhas and Masters all along will also be clear. Otherwise, even if you understand the principles, this is still information outside the gate, not really experience inside the house of Buddhas and Masters. Therefore you should realize that verbal expressions have a lot of subtleties.

In olden times a monk asked Xuefeng, "How is it when the spring is cold in the ancient valley?"

Xuefeng said, "When you look directly, you don't see the bottom."

The monk asked, "How about one who drinks from it?"

Xuefeng said, "It doesn't go in through the mouth."

The monk quoted this to Zhaozhou. Zhaozhou said, "It can't go in through the nose!"

The monk then asked Zhaozhou, "How is it when the spring is cold in the ancient valley?"

Zhaozhou said, "Painful."

The monk asked, "How about one who drinks from it?"

Zhaozhou said, "He dies."

When Xuefeng heard of this, he said, "Zhaozhou is an ancient Buddha; I bow to him from afar. From now on I won't give any more answers."

Look—Xuefeng, Great Master of True Enlightenment, had the foremost Zen eyes of his time; the masters Yunmen, Xuansha, Changqing, and Baofu all emerged from his school.[17] Nevertheless, when he

---

17. For speeches of Xuefeng, see "The House of Yun-men" in *The Five Houses of Zen;* for koans of Xuefeng, see *The Blue Cliff Record,* cases 5, 22, 49, 51; *Book of Serenity,* cases 24, 50, 55; *Unlocking the Zen Koan,* case 13. For speeches of Yunmen, see "The House of Yun-men" in *The Five Houses of Zen;* for koans of Yunmen, see *The Blue Cliff Record,* cases 6, 8, 14, 15, 22, 27, 34; *Book of Serenity,* cases 11, 40, 82, 92, 99; *Unlocking the Zen Koan,* cases 15, 16, 21, 39. For speeches of Xuansha, see "The House of Fa-yen" in *The Five Houses of Zen;* for koans of Xuansha, see *The Blue Cliff Record,* cases 22 and 88; *Book of Serenity,* case 81. For koans of Chanqing and Baofu, see *The Blue Cliff Record,* cases 8, 22, 23, 95.

heard Zhaozhou's answer, he bowed at a distance and stopped giving answers of his own accord. What was that all about! Do you think that's "flavorless"? Do you think it is meaningless? Do you think it is up to Xuefeng's state, or beyond Xuefeng's state? If you really know this deep meaning, you yourself can walk hand in hand with Xuefeng.

When Sushan heard a single example of a saying from the master of Mount Dayu, he bowed from afar and said, "The ancient Buddha of Mount Dayu radiates light reaching all the way here."

The moment the Hermit of Lotus Peak heard it said that "a gentleman likes wealth but gets it in a principled way," he said in astonishment, "A descendant of Yunmen still exists!" In the middle of the night he lit incense and bowed toward Yunju.[18]

Tell me, if these were flavorless or meaningless, who wouldn't be able to say them? Now as I look around, those who know how to be insipid, those who know how to pick pockets in broad daylight, and those who know how to be mindless are extremely common: as soon as they are questioned, they shout, or beat, or vomit sayings, or mime. If Xuefeng and Sushan were alive today, even if you bowed east to them every morning and bowed south to them every evening, you'd never be finished! Even if there were such people as Xuefeng and Sushan, what would be exceptional about them?

Also, you can't say there was no one in antiquity but there is now. Don't make the mistake of passing them by in vain so you get nothing from them—with clear faith that sayings have a lot of meaning, examine them closely for resolution. If you don't understand each and every one of all of these differentiations clearly and completely, even if your eyes are empty as space and your spunk swallows the universe, you are still a wild fox-spirit haunting the wilds.

18. On "the Hermit of Lotus Peak," see *The Blue Cliff Record*, case 25.

For this reason, National Teacher Daito said in a Japanese verse,[19]

> For more than thirty years now
> I too have lived in a fox cave;
> Now even the transformed human
> Has become civilized.

19. As Torei's discourse is written entirely in *kanbun*, the type of literary Chinese written in Japan, sometimes called Sino-Japanese, the transcription of this vernacular verse in the archaic usage prior to the invention of the Japanese writing systems, using Chinese characters in a mixture of semantic and phonetic applications, creates effects with nuances for Japanese people that cannot be reproduced in translation.

[6]

PROGRESSIVE TRANSCENDENCE

Here there is the path of progressive individual expression. This is called the experience that the ancestral teachers did not transmit. Therefore Banshan said, "The road beyond has not been transmitted by a thousand sages; students playing with forms are like monkeys grasping at reflections."

This is also called the last word. Fushan said, "At the last word you finally reach an unyielding barrier."

The guiding message is not in verbal explanation: what Buddhas and Masters since ancient times have received successively from one another unerringly has in every case been this one experience. Even if Zen monks truly investigate the mysterious subtleties thoroughly, pass through multiple barriers, and see through impenetrable stories going beyond, and yet stumble by this little task, it is for no other reason than that their vows of compassion are not profoundly serious and their will and attitude are not lofty and transcendent, their repentance is not sincere and their doubt is not thorough. As ever, they stay in their old habits.

For this reason ancients like National Teacher Shoitsu temporarily set up three fundamentals—principle, functions, and progression—to remedy this decadence.[1] Ever since the Middle Ages people have analyzed sayings to classify them as aids to intellectual understanding. What they don't realize is that your experiences of seeing nature are all principle, the sayings of Bud-

---

1. These were three categories of koans, later refined into five in Hakuin's school. For instructions of Shoitsu, see *The Original Face*.

dhas and Masters that are hard to understand are all functions, and in the experience of progressive transcendence are indications of having a life beyond. The reason our Zen school crowns all the schools is precisely because of transmitting this bit. If simply seeing nature clearly were to be considered enough, what need would there have been to set up our school besides?

Consider the great congregation on Spirit Mountain.[2] Do you think it was easy to get there? Everyone had been through repeated refinement and was completely fulfilled in principle and fact, in nature and characteristics. Do you think their understanding and knowledge were inferior to yours? Obviously you cannot match them. Now since they were like this, why was Reverend Kasyapa the only one to break into a smile? Ananda also attended the Buddha for thirty years, and his understanding at the Surangama assembly in particular was extremely deep,[3] and yet he didn't understand—why did he go to Kasyapa for transmission of this teaching?

In the present time, students think it's easy. They don't consider ancient precedents such as these. After studying some Zen, they waste their lives at leisure. How sad! The school of Bodhidharma is extinct!

Some say that the school of Bodhidharma was direct pointing to the human mind, seeing its nature, and becoming enlightened, so how could there be any principle beyond seeing nature? This may be so as far as it goes, unfortunately, but tell me, if Bodhidharma's teaching was only on seeing nature, why were there differences of skin, flesh, bones, and marrow?[4] Do you suppose he was cheating people?

---

2. This is one of the founding stories of Zen, the story of the flower and the smile. See *Transmission of Light*, case 2; and *Unlocking the Zen Koan*, case 6.

3. This refers to the *Surangama-sutra* or *Heroic Progress Scripture*, which became very influential among Chinese Zen Buddhists of the Song dynasty.

4. This refers to a story encapsulating Bodhidharma's evaluations of his four successors: one had gotten his skin, one his flesh, one his bones, and one his marrow. The main streams of transmission of Zen traditionally trace themselves to the last of these, the disciple who got the marrow.

When Baizhang first had his nose twisted by Mazu, he saw through clearly; why then is there the story of his second inquiry?[5] He told an assembly, "Buddhism is not a small matter. In the past I was deafened for three days by one shout from Mazu." When Zhang Wujin was reading Xuedou's citations of precedents,[6] coming to the story of Baizhang calling on Mazu, he said, "Highly refined pure gold won't change color." Tossing aside the book, he said, "If it were really like this says, how could Linji exist today?" And he composed a verse saying,

Mazu's one shout at Great Hero Peak—
The sound goes into his skull, deafened for three
    days.
When Huangbo heard this, he stuck out his tongue;
In Jiangxi they established the style of the school
    from this.

Later he said to Yuanwu, "I used to dislike Xuedou's presentation of Baizhang's saying he was deafened for three days, and I said, 'Highly refined pure gold wouldn't change color.' I have clearly realized that I didn't understand the true school of Jiangxi."

Yuanwu said, "I recently wrote a verse on it with precisely the same meaning as yours."

Wujin said, "Can I hear it?"

Yuanwu recited,

Standing up the whisk and hanging up the whisk,[7]
The whole works appears and disappears.
"At one with this or detached from it?"

---

5. See *The Blue Cliff Record*, cases 11 and 53.

6. This collection of citations with Xuedou's verse comments is the core of *The Blue Cliff Record*, which consists of Yuanwu's introductions, comments, and lectures on each example.

7. The handling of the fly-whisk is used symbolically to represent all functions, hence with picking it up and hanging it up, "The whole works appears and disappears."

His speech seems to draw a line.
Thunder rumbles right from the crown,
Needling out the fatal disease.
Deaf for three days taking on a shout,
If the lion cub's spiritual power unleashed a
     counterattack,
Even pure gold refined a hundred times would lose
     its color.

Wujin was pleased. He said, "I had always been afraid the path of the masters had weakened, but now I can say I've seen a master statesman in monk's garb. Luckily there is some reason beyond."

Linji, for another example, was greatly enlightened first at sixty strokes of the cane from Huangbo, but then he also associated with him for twenty years, throwing himself into a living forge, to be smelted a hundred times and refined a thousand times. Finally he climbed the mountain in the middle of summer retreat, stayed a few days, and then took his leave.

Huangbo said, "You broke the summer retreat to come here; now you're leaving without finishing the summer." Linji said, "I came for a while to pay respects to you." Huangbo then chased him away. After he'd gone a mile or so, Linji began to have some doubts about this, so he went back and finished the summer retreat.

One day he took leave of Huangbo. Huangbo asked, "Where are you going?" Linji said, "If not south of the river, I'll wind up north of the river." Huangbo then hit him. Linji grabbed and held him and gave him a slap. Huangbo roared with laughter and called to his attendant, "Bring my late teacher Baizhang's meditation brace and desk." Linji said, "Attendant, bring fire." Huangbo said, "Although you're right, just take them and go—later on you'll cut off the tongues of everyone on earth."

Now tell me, what was this all about? Nowadays people usually say, "His thieving mind had not yet died." Ha, ha! If you waste time this way, some day you'll have regrets.

Yunmen said, "To have no trouble at all in the world is an expression of transition; even when you are able to not see a single form, this is but half the issue. You must also know that there is a time when the whole issue is brought up, above and beyond."

Sushan said, "Before the Xiantong era, I knew what pertains to the reality body; after the Xiantong era, I knew what is beyond the reality body."[8]

We are fortunate to have such examples of people of old; why not be thorough? Take the likes of Xuedou's verses on one hundred examples—with each one he wanted to transmit this bit to descendants. In fact, all seventeen hundred koans are information on this little bit. Within them are the near and the far, the crude and the fine, the complete and the incomplete, in order to test whether or not you recognize this little bit. Therefore *The Blue Cliff Record* says,

> Jade is tested with water; gold is tested with a stone; a sword is tested with a hair; water is tested with a staff. In the school of patch-robe monks, with each word, each phrase, each act, each state, each exit, each entry, each greeting, each response, you need to see the shallow and the deep, you need to see whether someone is facing forward or backward.

In the present time there are some genuine patch-robed ones who bring great doubt to bear on sayings for years, according to the model of the ancients; when the time comes and their work has matured, one day they suddenly realize enlightenment. Because what they attain emerges out of the ancients' stories of the final end, they already think they know it. What they still don't realize is that this is an event along the way.

For example, the story of Zhaozhou's dog basically clearly presents the task of progressive transcendence, no small matter;[9]

---

8. "The Xiantong era" of the Tang dynasty lasted from 860 to 874, so the implication is that it took a long time for Sushan to make this progress.

9. For this story, see *Unlocking the Zen Koan*, case 1; *Book of Serenity*, case 18. The version typically used in the Rinzai schools says a monk asked the master, "Does a dog have buddha-nature or not?" The master said, "No."

even so, when students first study this story and suddenly penetrate, they have only reached the gate—this is just temporarily borrowing the empowerment of the saying to gain access to the ground of essential nature; it is not yet complete knowledge of the most profound meaning.

Simply because people have turned away from awareness and gotten involved in objects since beginningless time, their habits of confusion are deeply ingrained, and so when they come to find out this transcending Zen, everything they attain pertains to the process. This is why I have to distinguish this and put it in its place, repeating carefully, intent on pointing out the essentials of Zen. Let the knowledgeable try to get it themselves.

Yantou said, "Even the great Deshan doesn't know the last word." He also said, "I regret that I didn't tell him the last word at the start; had I told him, no one would be able to do anything to him."[10] Tell me, what is this principle? If there were no significance at all, would he have said these words?

But don't interpret a koan logically and think that's what it is. To seek this in koans is very far off; you have to pass through to liberation on the koan before you get it. Zen Master Wuzu Fayan first studied with Yuanzhao Ben and understood all the stories, ancient and contemporary. Next he saw Fushan Yuanjian, who told him, "Buddha had a secret saying; Kasyapa didn't conceal it." Wuzu's doubts then melted away. Later he studied with Baiyun.

One day he cited the story of a monk asking Nanquan about the wish-fulfilling jewel, and wanted to ask a question about it. Baiyun scolded him, and Wuzu attained enlightenment, breaking out in a sweat all over.

Not long after, Baiyun had Wuzu fill the post of head of the mill. One day Baiyun went to the mill and talked to Wuzu. "Do you know something?" he said.

"No," said Wuzu.

10. *Unlocking the Zen Koan,* case 13.

Baiyun said, "Recently several Zen travelers came from Mount Lu. All of them have experienced enlightenment, and when I have them explain Zen, they can explain it; they can also comment aptly and also compare and criticize past and present."

Wuzu said, "How did you deal with them?"

Baiyun said, "I told them they simply weren't there yet."

Wuzu felt great doubt about this. He thought to himself, "Since they've been enlightened, and can explain and understand, how is it that they're not there yet?" He went on wondering for days on end, to the point where food and drink had no flavor. Seven days later he finally realized what this meant, and all at once he let go of what he had hitherto treasured.

He ran to see Baiyun. Baiyun was overjoyed for him, but Wuzu just laughed once, that's all.

Wuzu always told this story to students, noting, "Because of this, I broke out in a sweat all over. From this I understood the 'clear wind after unloading.'"

He also said to the community, "I traveled for fifteen years. First I called on Master Xian and got the hair. Next I met an old adept at Sihai and got the skin. Then I went to the elder Fushan Yuanjian and got the bones. Subsequently at Master Baiyun's place I got the marrow. Only then did I presume to accept transmission and work as a teacher of others."[11]

See how he went through so many difficult straits before he was fit to be called a great teacher. Worthy of esteem, reviver of the Linji school, if he had not done all he did, would his descendants exist today?

I now tell you clearly: even if you realize your essential nature and understand koans, and can explain Zen and comment in conformity with the school of the masters and cleverly compare the false and true of past and present, when you get here you still haven't even dreamed of it. What is this principle? When your search reaches this point, you need to have some clarity.

---

11. For teachings of Fushan, see *Zen Lessons*, cases 9–17. For Wuzu's teachings, see *Zen Lessons*, cases 8–28; and "Zen Master Wuzu" in *Zen Essence*.

National Teacher Daio studied with Xutang. When Daio was going to return to Japan, Xutang sent him off with a verse:

Knocking at the door of the school,
Where the road ended, he kept going,
Clearly telling Old Man Xutang
His descendants over the Eastern Sea
Would increase with the passing days.

Tell me, what does this refer to? Why did he accept the prediction of increase with the passing days? People have no idea where this comes from and mistakenly call it inconceivable.

Once he had knocked on the door of the school of the Buddhas and Masters and figured it out in detail, reviewing thousands and thousands of times, studying all the Zen that can be studied, understanding all the teachings that can be understood, penetrating all the sayings that can be penetrated, now what would he study? When you can't find anything at all to investigate, that is called the end of the road. If he had stopped there, what would have been so good about Daio?

For this reason, National Teacher Kanzan's final admonitions say,

A long time ago our ancestor Daio braved the hardships of wind and waves to go to China early on. He met old Zen Master Xutang at Jingci, studied sincerely, and had genuine realization. Later he completed the esoterica at Jinshan. That is why he got praised for going on when the road ends and received the prediction that descendants would increase day by day. The unalloyed transmission of the orthodox lineage of Yangqi to our country was the achievement of our great ancestor.[12]

You should know this is very significant.

---

12. The Yangqi sect is a branch of the Linji school. See "Zen Master Yangqi" in *Zen Essence*; and "Facing Suchness" in *Teachings of Zen*. The other sect, called Huanglong, was introduced into Japan earlier by Eisai but did not flourish like the Yangqi lineage.

National Teacher Daito first studied with Bukkoku. Through genuine seeking and unalloyed effort, one night he was suddenly greatly enlightened. In the middle of the night he knocked at Bukkoku's door to present his insight. Bukkoku said, "This is genuine insight. You should set up the banner of Dharma and establish a school."

After that Daito heard Daio's methods were very harsh, and he headed to Kyoto and went directly to Daio's place. As they exchanged questions and answers back and forth, Daio didn't agree with him at all.

Then Daio posed the question, "Wuzu said to Foyan,[13] 'An ox goes through a window lattice: head, horns, and four hooves all get out; why can't the tail get out?' You try to make a statement." National Teacher Daito commented, "Divining with a ladle, he listens to the empty sound." Daio said, "Now that's something like it."

Thereafter Daito sought instruction morning and evening, not daring to regress. Daio also presented him with the saying, "Are Cuiyan's eyebrows still there? Yunmen said, 'A barrier!'"[14] Daito commented, "He adds error to error." Daio said, "You're right, but if you can focus on the word *barrier*, someday you'll have a life beyond."

Later he suddenly penetrated the word *barrier*. Sweat ran all down his back. He hurried to the teacher's room and made the comment, "Nearly the same way." Daio was very much surprised. He said, "Last night I dreamed Yunmen came to my room, and today you've gotten through his word *barrier*. You're a second coming of Yunmen!" Daito covered his ears and left.

The next day he presented two verses:

Once I passed through the cloud barrier,[15]
South, north, east, west, the living road was clear.

---

13. Foyan was one of the so-called Three Buddhas among Wuzu's disciples. For his lectures, see *Instant Zen*.

14. *The Blue Cliff Record*, case 8.

15. The name *Yunmen* means "cloud gate."

Lodging by night, traveling by day, neither guest nor
host,
My feet arouse a pure breeze underfoot.

On passing through the cloud barrier, the former
road's not there:
Under the blue sky in broad daylight, this is my
home mountain.
The wheel of potential gets through and changes,
hard for people to reach;
The golden ascetic gives up and goes home.

Daio picked up a brush to write an afterword: "You accord in
both light and darkness: I am not as good as you. With you, our
school will flourish. But mature for twenty years before you let
people know of this testimony."

That Zen Master Bukkoku was greatly admired by Bukko and
was parent to Muso;[16] how could he have easily spoken words of approval? The fact is that Daito was already clearly enlightened; he just
lacked a bit. When he came into the presence of Daio, his realization
was like a shadow, like a puddle compared to an ocean, like a hair in
the immense sky, like an ant trying to shake an iron pillar, a mos-
quito in a gale. Shouldn't he be happy? Who wouldn't seek this?[17]

I first experienced distinct clarity on Lotus Blossom Mountain
in the province of Omi, but when I later went to the cave of the
Incorrigible [Hakuin],[18] I couldn't even open my mouth. Thence-
forth I lowered my head from the clouds and sought instruction
morning and evening.

---

16. Bukkoku (1241–1316) was the teacher of the great Muso Soseki (1275–1351),
who was named national teacher by seven emperors. Some of his dialogues were
published in his own time, eventually becoming one of the native classics of
Japanese Zen. See *Dream Conversations* for a translation of this key work.

17. That is, he should be happy to realize his incompleteness and have an opportunity for further enlightenment.

18. "The Incorrigible" (Sanskrit, *icchantika*) was one of Hakuin's pen names,
an ironic reference to compassion.

One day my teacher said, "Suppose a powerful devil came up behind you and reached out and grabbed you and threw you into a blazing pit of fire. At this point, would you have any way out?" At that time I was unable to get up and leave my teacher's room; I was so ashamed that I sweat all over. After that, whenever I went to his room, the teacher asked, "Do you have a way out?" I could never answer. If I had been like you folks, with your easy-going attitude, couldn't I have answered with an action or an object? Because I deeply respect and believe in the significance of being thorough, I never said anything to cover up.

Now I was uneasy all the time. Even the universe seemed cramped; the sun and moon seemed dark. In the spring of the next year, 1744, I asked to retire into seclusion to seek thoroughness day and night.

The teacher came one day and said, "The stereotype of the stalwart is before you. Don't be afraid of the stereotype; just find out the source of the stereotype. This is why it is said that the ancients worried about dying without reviving, while people today worry about reviving and so don't die.

"It's like falling into the water. Only when you reach bottom can you come up as soon as your feet touch. If you're so afraid of sinking that you flail wildly with your hands and feet, your whole body will tire out and you'll drown.

"This is called letting go over a steep cliff, then after perishing, returning to life. You must be thorough."

When I heard these words, it was like swallowing ghee. From this point on my work was greatly strengthened, and I spurred myself on all the more.

Subsequently I read the *Diamond sutra* for several days and suddenly attained absorption in transcendent insight, to the point where I forgot body and mind.[19] Then in order to test this, I also read the section [of the *Flower Ornament-sutra*] on the practical vows of Universal Good,[20] and got some knowledge of

19. For a Zen commentary on the *Diamond-sutra*, see *The Sutra of Hui-neng: Grand Master of Zen*.
20. *The Flower Ornament Scripture*, pp. 1503–18.

the Flower Ornament cosmos. Next I read the *Lotus-sutra*,[21] and coming to the section of life span, I suddenly realized the *Lotus samadhi* and saw all the teachings of Buddha's whole lifetime, as if I were seeing them in the palm of my hand.

I ran to tell the teacher, "I've wanted to read the canon for a long time, but never finished. Now I see through it at a glance." The teacher said, "Good! This happiness of yours is like the tower-climbing story of the ministry president Chen Cao.[22] How do you understand it?"

I told him truthfully. The teacher said, "Be conscientious." He also said, "Speaking for the official, how would you please the ministry president?" I tried several sayings, but none satisfied him. The next day in an interview I managed to present a saying that made the teacher get up unconsciously and hit me twice; he said, "You've finally managed to say something satisfactory. Even so, don't take it easy. Later on you'll come to know on your own."

The next day I again went for an interview. The teacher asked, "How do you understand the story of Sushan's memorial tower?" I said, "He wants to cut off people's root of life with a poisonous hand." The teacher said, "What about after cutting off the root of life—precisely what is that life?" I said, "Sushan and the craftsman put forth a hand together."[23] The teacher said, "You're

---

21. The popular name of the influential *Saddharmapundarika-sutra*, favored by the Tendai school.

22. *The Blue Cliff Record*, commentary to case 33.

23. When Sushan's memorial tower was to be built, the administrator came and told him. Sushan said, "How much are you going to pay the craftsman?" The administrator said it was up to Sushan. Sushan said, "Should you give him three *wen*, two *wen*, or one *wen*? If you can say, you build me the memorial tower yourself." The administrator was at a loss. At the time Master Luoshan was living on Mount Dayu. A monk came telling this story, and Luoshan asked if anyone had been able to answer. The monk replied in the negative, so Luoshan told him, "You go back and tell Sushan that if he pays the craftsman three *wen*, he'll never get a monument in this life; if he pays the craftsman two *wen*, he and the craftsman together will put forth a single hand; if he pays the craftsman one *wen*, he'll get the craftsman in trouble, and his eyebrows and beard will fall out." When this was related to Sushan, he bowed to Luoshan

not through yet." I then also cited the story of Zhaozhou exposing the woman and said, "If I had been there, I'd have said to Zhaozhou, 'Did you expose her before speaking or after speaking?'" The teacher said in Zhaozhou's stead, "Go right ahead." I said, "Then the woman of Taishan has been exposed by you." The teacher abruptly asked, "Where do you meet the woman of Taishan?"[24] As I tried to say, the teacher changed his expression and said in a harsh voice, "No, no—that's not it."

The next day when I went for an interview, on seeing me coming, the teacher hurriedly stuck out his hand and said, "How does my hand resemble Buddha's hand?" I came up with a saying immediately, and the teacher praised it highly. I then said, "You recently asked about the story of the woman burning the hut.[25] At the time I missed the woman's subtle skill. Saying what she did, the woman couldn't but shock the monk into a depression and puzzle everyone on earth to death. I have a saying on behalf of the hermit; I'd grab the woman and say, 'I've been receiving your support for twenty years.'" Before I had even finished, the teacher drew himself up and shouted so loud the sound penetrated my marrow. My chest hurt for several days, and my body and mind were in a daze, as if I were in a haze. I thought to myself, "I've attained enlightenment clearly—why am I like this? It must be that even though I have the eye to see nature, my power of meditation concentration is not yet mature."

At this, I vowed to try to perfect meditation concentration, but as the days and months came and went, as ever I was still not free. Subsequently I went into seclusion, where I could not be reached, and struggled day and night, just like a condemned man counting the days till his execution.

---

at a distance, saying, "On Mount Dayu is an old Buddha who radiates light reaching here. Even so, this is a lotus in the winter." When this was reported to Luoshan, he said, "My speaking thus was already growing several more yards of turtle hair."

24. *Unlocking the Zen Koan,* case 31; *Book of Serenity,* case 10.

25. A woman supported a hermit for twenty years. One day she sent a young woman to test him, and the hermit rebuffed her coldly. The woman who supported him said he was after all a worldly man and burned down his hut.

Mightily manipulating the pearl of awareness, I didn't put it down for an instant. Sometimes getting it, sometimes losing it, I found correct mindfulness hard to keep continuous. Sorrow and apprehension clogged my chest, and I was uneasy whether sitting down, or up and about.

This went on for half a hundred days, when suddenly all fell into place. Shattering the luminous pearl, completely bare, totally naked, I truly understood the "clear wind after unloading."

Even so, my application was not yet thoroughgoing. So I whipped the dead ox again to forge ahead nonstop. Gritting my teeth and clenching my fists, I didn't notice I had a body. Even on freezing days and frigid nights my clothing was always moist with sweat. Sometimes when the demon of sleep was strong I stuck myself with a needle. Penetrating bone and marrow, finding no taste in food and drink, I passed another half a hundred days. During that time I had insights eight or nine times, and on the last day I saw through my teacher's everyday experience. Ah, ha, ha! The dead work I had mistakenly been doing, along with the white clouds, deserved thirty strokes of the cane.

I knew in truth my teacher's empowerment was tremendous— if he hadn't led me along and instructed me so much, how could I be where I am today? I would have spent my whole life mistakenly remaining dead within understanding and knowledge. Now as I think of past events, every word, every phrase, was dripping with blood, frightening and saddening. Ever since then, my mindfulness has been uninterrupted. I studied day and night, never stopping. How can we waste time idly with an easygoing attitude?

I want to practice this path diligently to revive the true Way, now in decline, as best I can. Don't you want this too? When it comes to this, please have a single eye.

Because I've had many illnesses, I am able to recognize others' illnesses. As I have cured my illnesses, I've also learned about medicines. As my illnesses were gradually cured, then I worried about others' illnesses. Because others had illnesses, my illness recurred. Zen Master Luopu said, "At the last word you finally come to the hard and fast barrier." How true these words are! Passing through birth and death to liberation, wielding the stamp of truth, is all in reference to this time: only by taking on the highest function will you become expert. I too am like this: I only want there to be someone like this three thousand miles away to cure this illness of mine. But if not, then let everyone in the world criticize freely.

[7]

WORKING APPLICATION

People may be of the present or the past, but the Way has no past or present. A person can practice the Way, but on attainment of the Way, the person is forgotten. Therefore the Way is the person; there is no person besides. So it is said that if the Way is the same as of old, so is the person. The only reason for not being equal to the ancients is that perception of the Way is not transcendent, and practical application is not clear.

Now that you know the experience beyond, you need to put it into practice clearly. Mention of seeking continuity of right mindfulness refers to this time. Great Master Bodhidharma said, "Many understand the Way, but few practice it." Master Dong-shan said, "Continuity is very difficult." Shoju Rojin said, "It's hard to find even one in ten thousand who has continuous correct mindfulness."

When Diamond Navel Bodhisattva was practicing the Way long ago, a demon king followed him for a thousand years, looking for his tracks, and never could find them. And Master Dong-shan lived in a cloister all his life, and the earth spirit wanted to get a glimpse of him but never was able to do so. These are ancient models of continuity of correct mindfulness.

Even so, if one does not transmit the bit of progressive transcendence, that's really making a living in a ghost cave. And even if you know the transcendental, if your practical application isn't clear, you are just one who embraces the Way and still cannot exercise great function.

For this reason, though there have been quite a few people with accurate insight, those among them who attained the great function of great potential were rare. Zen Master Huangbo said, "Mazu had eighty-four successors who presided over places of practice, but there were only three or four who got Master Ma's true eye."

Zen Master Lingyuan Qing used to tell students, "It's hard to find authentic people in Zen schools. After leaving Huitang, the only genuine Zen master I saw was my Dharma brother on East Mountain."[1]

Zen Master Dahui said, "Of the venerable adepts in old Nan's line, Wuzu only agreed with two elders, Huitang and Zhenjing, that's all. The rest he didn't accept."[2]

Also, Ying-an said, "Haven't you seen how Master Dasui said, 'I called on more than seventy teachers, and only one or two had great perception. The rest all had accurate insight.'"

Right now the only real teacher in the world with great perception is my Dharma uncle and old teacher [Hakuin]. His black-lacquered bamboo wand overturns oceans and mountains, striking through from the start; though it is medicine for a dead horse, it is the quintessence thereof.

Also, Master Chijue said, "I traveled in monastic society for thirty years; in those days the only one with great perception was old Songyuan. If he hadn't been that way, how could Buddhism have survived until today?"[3]

You should know that there is another lock on this. But each and every one of those teachers of ancient times all have knowledge and function beyond convention; the selection of one or two like this is only about having tremendous vision. Teachers in the present time do not have the perception to distinguish objectively. They wrongly criticize people of old for not realizing

1. For teachings of Huitang, see *Zen Lessons*, cases 35–40; for Lingyuan, see *Zen Lessons*, cases 64–79. "East Mountain" refers to Wuzu Fayan; see *Zen Lessons*, cases 17–28.

2. "Old Nan" refers to Huanglong Huinan, after whom the Huanglong sect of the Linji school is named. For Huanglong Huinan's teaching, see *Zen Lessons*, cases 41–47, and "Zen Master Huanglong" in *Zen Essence*.

3. For teachings of Chijue, see *Teachings of Zen*, pp. 109–14. For Songyuan, see *Teachings of Zen*, pp. 105–7.

their own errors, and they mistakenly claim their way surpasses the ancients. That's laughable. Leaving aside for the moment those specifically indicated by Huangbo and the others, what about the rest of those known as Zen masters—do you think they can even be spoken of on the same day as the "enlightened teachers" of the present time? Their virtue moved the age; the dragons and elephants of the whole land were all influenced by them. Therefore you should realize that the ancestral teachers' selections of people were the most difficult of difficulties, the most subtle of subtleties.

In olden times Guishan asked Yangshan, "Of Mazu's eighty-four successors, how many attained great potential and how many attained great function?" Yangshan said, "Baizhang attained great potential; Huangbo attained great function. The rest were just guides."[4]

Look—the descendants of our Linji each had capability beyond a teacher and never died at a saying of a teacher of the school.[5] After a thousand hardships and myriad pains entering bones and penetrating marrow, everything flowed from their own hearts. With this, they put forth a single hand together to support the true Way. This is why the way of Zen continued and did not die out.

In olden times it was said that Yunmen saved with words while Linji saved with acts.[6] The truth is not so. Even if you have the marvelous exposition of a Yunmen, without the great workings of a Linji it is like having the status of an emperor without the power of a general. The resulting deterioration winds up degenerating into mysterious vagueness, and mysterious vagueness turns into subtle slipperiness. Everyone after the great Ben was like this.[7]

---

4. For Baizhang, Guishan, and Yangshan, see "The House of Kuei-Yang" in *The Five Houses of Zen*. For Huangbo, see "The House of Lin-chi" in *The Five Houses of Zen*.

5. In Zen parlance, to "die at a saying" means to stop at a partial understanding and stagnate mentally.

6. For Yunmen, see "The House of Yun-men" in *The Five Houses of Zen*.

7. This refers to Shanben, a highly distinguished master in the sixth generation of the Yunmen school. His teacher was a successor to Xuedou, the author of the poetic commentaries on koans that form the core of *The Blue Cliff Record*.

Then again, if you have the great workings of a Linji, without the marvelous exposition of a Yunmen, it's like having the power of a general without the rank of an emperor; the resulting deterioration winds up degenerating into inaccessible oddity, and inaccessible oddity turns into crude forcefulness.

The Zen types of the present day are generally no better than this, but the likes of Yunmen and Linji were not like this at all. They were able to transcend beyond great workings and marvelous exposition, and also sported within great workings and marvelous exposition. When their schools degenerated, they took the traces of that sporting and made them into stereotypes. Therefore our Linji, from the time of the masters Xinghua and Fengxue, was also equipped with Yunmen's marvelous exposition; the style of the school changed, and Buddhism was renewed daily.[8]

Based on this, Great Master Wuzu came riding on the wheel of vows and reopened the school of East Mountain, singing the song of Yunmen and wielding the sword of Linji, like two wheels of a chariot. The way of the school, well established, revived the authentic lineage of the Buddhas and Masters, therefore causing their heritage not to die out. Zhenjing had a verse that said,

> Yunmen and Linji—a spring of a hundred flowers;
> Everyone with spiritual potential had genius.

If they all had genius, wouldn't springtime return to the garden of the masters? Henceforth Yuanwu, Huqiu, Ying-an, and Mi-an successively appeared in the world and labored to practice this path and revive the way of the school.

For this reason, when Songyuan was dying, he said to the community, "Among those who travel the right road there are those who are unable to use the written teachings. The path of Linji is on the verge of dying out. What a pity!" Xutang cited

---

8. Linji's assistant Xinghua is cited briefly in *Book of Serenity*, case 35. For classic commentaries on koans featuring Fengxue, see *The Blue Cliff Record*, cases 38 and 61; and *Book of Serenity*, cases 29 and 34.

this and said, "The old teacher of Vulture Peak seems much like he's mounting a horse with the help of a staff—though there's no danger of falling, he can't avoid looking ridiculous to onlookers. Tsk!" Even the great Xutang was affected by Songyuan's poison and also wanted to hurt others, as a result afflicting our first patriarch of Zen in Japan, with the calamity extending to his posterity. If Shoju Rojin had not labored for forty years to distinguish this poison ingredient, descendants of later generations would be hopeless.

What time is this? Who can take the responsibility? Please set the eye on your forehead high and practice this path diligently to revive the true Way, now in decline, and not let its posterity die out.

This section on working application is most important. Revival of the true school and circulation of true perception are all in this. Even so, since the final direction is not in verbal explanation, how can this be discussed in words? Wrong, wrong! It just takes people of great power to pick up the true school and carry it on one shoulder and not let the true way of Buddhas and Masters die out!

[8]

LEARNING FROM A TEACHER

Ever since the transcendent attainment fell to the ground, no one values learning from a teacher. Self-enlightened, with their own views, people argue over false and true, indulging their own portion of knowledge instead of basing it on the ancients.

In olden times, Zen Master Xuance of Dongyang visited Great Master Xuanjiao of Yongjia and had an intense discussion with him. Finding that his words unconsciously accorded with the patriarchs, Xuance asked, "Who is your Dharma teacher?" He said, "I've listened to discourses on the Universal scriptures and have transmission from a teacher for each one. Later I understood the Buddha-mind school through the scripture of Vimalakirti but have not yet had anyone confirm it." Xuance said, "That's all right 'before the prehistoric Buddha,' but those who are enlightened on their own 'after the prehistoric Buddhas' are all naturalist outsiders."[1]

Also, Master Ying-an said,

> The founder of Zen came from the West touting this thing in particular, only valuing comprehension outside of words, directly penetrating the heights and the depths. Why do you need to chant morning and evening on the edge of a meditation seat in order to call it Buddhism or the Way of Zen? That's actually blinding people. But you shouldn't abandon instruction from a teacher in order to seek on your own. Those who attain by seeking on their own are actually outsiders of one kind or another.

---

1. See "Key Events" in *The Sutra of Hui-neng: Grand Master of Zen*, pp. 56–57.

In the present time, being totally lacking in teaching heritage, perception is not completely refined, and everyone puts forth his own view when dealing with people, unconsciously blinding students. This goes on and on, from one to another, one blind person leading many blind people.

The matter of learning from a teacher is most essential. People of old who arrived at the source of seeing nature, passed through many barriers clearly and completely without a dot of doubt, and traveled freely through the world opening big mouths in discussion, only came to know the transcendental message of Zen after they finally ran into Zen masters of great vision. Then they sincerely sought certainty and wound up with the duty of the teacher's succession, bearing the debt of Dharma, never to forget it for a moment. This is called Dharma succession. Since ancient times the designated succession of the ancestral teachers has always been like this.

So Yunmen was greatly enlightened when Muzhou broke his leg,[2] but then went to Xuefeng, from whom he inherited the Dharma. There certainly was a reason for this.

When Longya was traveling, he clearly had perception. In order to test whether the old teachers everywhere had perception or not, he'd first make a point; even Suiwei and Linji couldn't contain him.[3] Later, when "the Dong River flowed backward," he finally turned around and recognized he'd been misapplying effort. Ultimately he succeeded to Dongshan. Later people didn't realize there is great significance to this issue, and based on Xutang's general talks, mistakenly said that Longya's application was the true meaning of transcendence. If you understand this way, where do you put "the Dong River flowed backward"?

What you don't realize is that Xutang spoke as he did fearing you'd misinterpret Longya as having no perception, wanting to let you know Xuedou versified it truly—even if he understood the living meaning of Zen, still on arriving here there's a life

---

2. *The Blue Cliff Record,* commentary to case 6.
3. *The Blue Cliff Record,* case 20.

beyond. For this reason he also paid respects to Longya's monument, saying in his eulogy, "Suiwei and Linji fell short in their ability; when the Dong River reversed its flow, only then did he reach home." This makes it clear that he only arrived at this home mountain where the Dong River ran backward because his previous understanding was not yet his real home.

The succession of the ancient worthies was always like this. People of the present time don't know the importance of succession and mistakenly make all sorts of arguments over and over. Therefore those who have no teacher's heritage should first seek out a great Zen master who has definitely succeeded to the Buddhas and Patriarchs, while those who do have a teacher's heritage should find out the teacher's innermost meaning. Once you have found out, then don't betray it.

In olden times, old Jiao of Kaisheng was first trained by Wuzu, but later he didn't trace his roots to this attainment and erroneously succeeded to Iron Legs Fu of Changlu. When he offered up incense to thank the latter, he suddenly developed a growth in his chest. It wouldn't heal, and he finally died.

Xiuyan was greatly enlightened first at Shimen's citation, but subsequently succeeded to Fozhao Guang. For this reason he was never at ease in his heart and would sometimes laugh, sometimes cry. His lectures were mostly like ditties. Sometimes he'd point to the other's portrait and say, "I was instructed by this old master; it's all because of failing in the duty of gratitude that I have brought on this painful consequence."

From time to time, those who do not know what teaching heritage is based on may pursue powerful positions or fall into human feelings. They go this way and that, like little people watching a game, going up and down along with the others. Sometimes there are those who have genuine realization but no heritage from a teacher; or they may have a teacher's heritage, but it is not a genuine transmission. An ancient said, "Buddha reached out to Buddha; master transmitted to master." In the present time it is not so; instead, the heritage of a teacher is taken to be a sign indicating abbacy. How can they know the deep meaning of the succession of Buddhas and Masters?

How great is our school! How deep is our Way! Even if you get it, it's hard to plumb. Even if you plumb it, it's hard to exhaust. Even if you've plumbed and exhausted it, its subtlety is hard to penetrate. In olden times Quan Dadao studied with Ciming. Ciming said, "A bit of cloud lies across the mouth of the valley; where does the traveler come from?" Quan looked around and said, "Last night fire from where burned out the ancients' tombs?" Ciming said, "Not yet—speak again." Quan made a tiger's roar. Ciming set out a seat cloth; Quan pushed him down onto the seat. Ciming also made a tiger's roar. Quan retreated and said with a laugh, "I've called on more than eighty teachers, and you are the only one who can continue the true school of Linji."

This is to be valued; not only did Ciming's attainment go beyond ordinary sense, he also spiked his thigh to succeed to the true school. If students hear of his manner, how could they not blush with embarrassment?

Baiyun one day in his room cited Yunmen's saying to an assembly, "Such big chestnuts—how many can you eat?" None of the group's comments fit. He asked Wuzu. Wuzu said, "He hangs out mutton but sells dog meat." Baiyun was startled at this. Wuzu once said, "After twenty years' study, I now know to be embarrassed." Later Lingyuan heard of this and said in praise, "Good words—*know to be embarrassed*," and composed a poem on true succession based on it, which was subsequently included among his works. At first there had been controversy between the Yangqi and Huanglong sects; it was in this context that Lingyuan Qing wrote a poem on the true succession of Wuzu, wherein he puts him forward as a true successor.[4]

When Zen Master Dahui heard of Ying-an's lecture at Golden Wheel Monastery, he was very pleased and said, "The main line of Yangqi is in this elder!" Subsequently he sent him the robe of true transmission and a verse. The verse said,

---

4. Lingyuan was a Huanglong master; Wuzu was a Yangqi master.

He sits occupying the foremost peak of Golden
  Wheel:
A thousand bogeys, a hundred monsters, all
  disappear.
Recently I've also gotten some news of reality;
I announce the true line of Yangqi comes through.

From this, Ying-an was considered to be the orthodox line. See how people of old spoke of authentic lineage time and again. Zen Master Dahui Zonggao had real Zen perception unique in his time. Xutang praised him: "There is no Sakyamuni before him, no Maitreya after him; in the heavens and the human world, there is no other like him." So then what was the reason he put Ying-an forward as the main line? Even among those who have equally succeeded to the true transmission from Buddhas and Patriarchs, the main line is even more extraordinary.

Just knowing that Buddhism is extremely deep and has this quintessence, first you should practice this path diligently. Even if you do so, it's still hard to find the true source. But if you don't, how can you help our school revive?

People of the present generation have not even dreamed of the deep meaning of the teacher's heritage; how could they know of this premise of the main line! But genuine high-minded students of the mystery will resolve injustice here!

[9]

MATURATION

Zen Master Yuanwu said,

Wearers of the patchwork robe should be intensely concerned about death and birth, and work diligently to dissolve barriers of knowledge, views, and interpretation, to thoroughly realize the great cause transmitted by the Buddhas and Patriarchs. Don't crave fame; step back and focus on truth. The more you conceal yourself, the more you should hide; it is the sages and celestials who will promote people.[1]

When the Sixth Patriarch had inherited the robe and gotten the Dharma, he disappeared into the South.[2]

After National Teacher Zhong of Nanyang received the mind-seal, he lived in a mountain valley for more than forty years without coming down the mountain, while his practice of the Way was heard of in the imperial capital.[3]

Nanquan rested his staff at Chiyang, built a meditation studio by himself, and his shadow did not leave the mountain for more than thirty years.[4]

1. The original letter of Yuanwu says, "The more you conceal yourself, the more you can't hide." Ancient masters became famous for their humility, and humbler in their fame.

2. See *Unlocking the Zen Koan*, case 23.

3. See *The Blue Cliff Record*, case 18; *Book of Serenity*, case 85; *Unlocking the Zen Koan*, case 17.

4. See *The Blue Cliff Record*, cases 28 and 31; *Book of Serenity*, cases 9, 69, 91; *Unlocking the Zen Koan*, cases 14 and 34; *The Pocket Zen Reader*, p. 103; *Teachings of Zen*, pp. 21–23.

Zen Master Fachang of Damei went to the old retreat of the Apricot Saint, where he fed on pine nuts and clothed himself in lotus leaves, and worked hard for thirty years.[5]

Master Fengxue used to beg in villages by day, then burn pine sap by night, staying on a single mat for seven years.

Master Fenyang, gesturing with his hands, said, "I worked as a gruel-and-rice monk for a long time before transmission of the Buddha's mind-seal. It is not a trivial job." He was invited to assume an abbacy eight times but insistently remained supine and did not respond.

Yangqi lived in a ramshackle place for twenty years, with "pearls of snow" filling the seats.[6]

The Fourth Grand Master concentrated his mind without sleeping for about sixty years.

Master Guishan spent several decades boiling chestnuts to eat; then in his later years Da-an came, and eventually fifteen hundred monks gathered.[7]

Master Ciming was a true model of diligence in Zen schools. At Fenyang he paid no mind to the bitter cold of the region; as he worked on the Way, he stuck his thigh with an awl to keep from falling asleep. His attainment of power came to fruition, and he became the Lion King of West River.

After National Teacher Daito finally received the old patriarch's mission of profound purity, he matured for twenty years and ultimately revealed the great and far-reaching high virtue of Daio.

After National Teacher Kanzan got the marrow of enlightenment from Daito, he went deep into the mountain valleys and cultivated refinement for twenty years. In the daytime he worked as a servant for commoners; by night he'd sit peacefully in a mountain cave.

---

5. See *Unlocking the Zen Koan,* case 30.

6. See *Record of Things Heard,* 4:14.

7. See "The House of Kuei-Yang" in *The Five Houses of Zen; The Blue Cliff Record,* cases 4, 24, 70; *Book of Serenity,* cases 37 and 60; *Unlocking the Zen Koan,* case 40.

The other enlightened teachers who hid here and there working intensely are too numerous to mention them all. Shoju Rojin, for example, abandoned social conventions, stopped all involvements, and worked hard for forty years. Even when invited by savants and lords, he didn't go; even when pressured by Zen monks, he didn't rise.

Once when villagers were being molested by wolves, for several days he surreptitiously went to the cremation and burial grounds here and there and sat peacefully through the night. When the wolves sniffed at his ears in annoyance, or snorted at his throat, he was intent on testing whether or not the continuity of his right mindfulness would be interrupted.

All those who forgot themselves for the Dharma were like this. Every one of the ancients since time immemorial was so. In some of them it was obvious; in others it was secret. Going deep into mountain forests, shutting off the mundane world, with reports of cultivation of the Way moving people's hearts, is what is called obvious seclusion. Nanyang and Lazy Can were examples of this.[8] As for continuity of right mindfulness regardless of time or place, without contamination of views, no one notices any evidence of it; this is called secret seclusion. Zhaozhou and Puhua were examples of this.[9]

As their habits were not the same and their practical affinities were individually different, some hid in mountain forests, some hid in the dust of the cities, some lived in monasteries, some lived alone. Some were obvious; some were covert.

It's like medicines curing diseases. When the disease is cured, the medicine is eliminated, and one puts oneself in others' positions; this is a description of how the people of old emerged in the world with expedients. Therefore, if you want to reach

---

8. For Nanyang, see *The Blue Cliff Record*, commentary to case 18. For Lazy Can, see *The Blue Cliff Record*, verse commentary to case 34.

9. For Zhaozhou, see *The Blue Cliff Record*, cases 2, 9, 30, 41, 45, 52, 57–59, 80, 96; *Book of Serenity*, cases 9, 18, 39, 47, 63; *Unlocking the Zen Koan*, cases 1, 7, 11, 14, 19, 31, 37; *Teachings of Zen*, pp. 33–34. Puhua was an odd monk who appears in the *Record of Linji*.

the realm realized by the ancients, you must thoroughly understand the foregoing principles, attain the experience that neither Buddhas nor Masters can transmit, without loss of the essential message of Zen or error in teaching heritage; *this* is what is to be developed to maturity.

Please cultivate the Way in this sense for many years, without fame and profit on your mind, without thoughts of money or valuables; you should want to help revive the true Way of Buddhas and Masters, which has collapsed. Yuanwu said, "After people of old had attained the Way, they lived boiling wild vegetable roots in broken-legged pots in huts or caves, never seeking fame or profit, being free and untrammeled, occasionally saying something to requite their debt to the Buddhas and Masters and transmit the seal of the Buddha-mind."

After Zen monks have finished the great task, the only rule for long years is maturing enlightenment, that's all. Don't rashly promote construction and insist on inviting students. When the ancients built temples and gathered people, they didn't do it because they themselves sought it, but when their work on the Way was fully mature and wearers of the patch robe came in increasing numbers, sanctuaries sprang up daily without their seeking them.

Yuanwu's *Essentials of Mind* says,

When Ciming took leave of Fenyang in olden times, Fenyang said in congratulating him, "There will naturally be people who will repair and build. As for you, you will be master of Buddhism." After that he was abbot at five major monasteries, but didn't move a single rafter; he just promoted the true school of Linji. Eventually he found three great men—Yangqi, Huanglong, and Cuiyan—and his descendants spread all over the land. In sum, he didn't violate the bequest he was given. Such was the seriousness with which the ancients chose capable people. In truth, magnificently arrayed and splendidly adorned sanctuaries are not sufficient grounds for considering Buddhism special.

Also, National Teacher Daito's final instructions say,

After my travels, some temples flourished, with buddha shrines and scriptures written in gold and silver, large congregations bustling with activity, some reciting scriptures or spells, sitting constantly without lying down, eating once a day before noon, carrying out observances six times a day. Even going on this way, they do not have at heart the sublime Way that even Buddhas and Masters cannot communicate, and they disregard cause and effect, so the real Way collapses. They are all devil's brood. After I'm long gone, they cannot claim to be my descendants. But if there is even one individual who practices in the wilds, under a handful of thatch, boiling wild vegetable roots in a broken-legged pot to get through the days, focusing solely on understanding self, this is someone who meets me every day and who shows gratitude. Who presumes to be contemptuous? Work on this. Work on this.

Please let this document be a reminder to develop maturity.

CIRCULATION

Communicating the teaching and liberating the living is the fundamental aim of the patch-robed monk. The great Nagarjuna said, "Even if you prostrate yourself for countless aeons or make your body into a seat for the whole universe, if you don't communicate the teaching and liberate the living, you cannot requite your debt."

Also, an ancient said, "What our school values is only communion with the source and communication by speech, having the tooth and nail of transcendence, and dissolving stickiness and removing bonds for people. This is called communicating the teaching to liberate the living. The rest is all trivia."

Now those to whom the transcendental has been communicated and who are continuing the way of Zen, which has already collapsed, should first of all think of requiting their debt to the Buddhas and Masters. What does it mean to requite debt? It means upholding the transcendental to teach one or two individuals with spiritual bones, enabling them to inherit this true school and disseminate it in the future, not allowing the sun of wisdom of the Buddhas and Masters to die out. If, however, they trail mud and drip water, putting up signposts and arranging clichés, making fools of people, that will never do.

Master Zhaozhou said, "If you would have me treat people according to their faculties and potentials, there are already the teachings of the three vehicles in twelve parts that have dealt with them—it's not up to me."

Master Xutang said,

Is there any comparison? Nowadays they occupy the seat of teaching illegitimately, using dogma to entrap students. They cultivate personnel with comfortable quarters, ambitiously aim for successorship by giving away clothing and food, trying to populate their schools by a series of inducements. How miserable! The voice of truth has died out! Since ancient times venerable adepts have tended to seek people on a sword's edge and even then could barely find anyone; how much the less by means of rules and regulations!

So the ancestral teachers from time immemorial who had great vision did not approve people easily. Look at Fayan's succession, for example. In his time he found many people, but I've never heard of any who continued his lineage generation after generation.[1] As for the school of Linji, from Xinghua and Nanyuan on, successors to their Dharma numbered only one or two in each case.[2] It's not that they lacked ability and couldn't liberate people; it was that they didn't approve people easily because their own powers were beyond other people. The likes of those nowadays who think big bustling congregations and flourishing temple establishments constitute a great prospering of Buddhism are truly ridiculous.

However, when it comes to the expedients with which the masters reached out, and the strategic adaptations of operations, you must seek within your own working application—do not seek from the words of others. Yantou said, "If you want to broadcast the Great Doctrine someday, let it all flow from your own heart to cover heaven and earth for others."

Please communicate in this way to seek successors to transmit it to the future so it will not die out. Buddhism is in peril, like piled eggs, and may become extinct.

1. This is not Wuzu Fayan, but Fayan Wenyi (885–958). See "The House of Fa-Yen" in *The Five Houses of Zen; Book of Serenity*, cases 17, 27, 51, 74; *Unlocking the Zen Koan*, case 26.

2. Nanyuan was a third-generation Linji master; he was the teacher of the more famous Fengxue, cited earlier in this work. See *The Blue Cliff Record*, commentary to case 38.

Suppose people are traveling in a wilderness and wild wind and violent rain extinguish their lamps, but then there is an individual whose only fear is that his lamp will go out, and shields it with his body left and right, paying no attention to anything else. The true lamp of Zen is like this: if you don't enable one or two authentic successors to perpetuate this true lamp, on what will descendants of later generations rely? Once their lamp in the wilderness in the dark of night goes out, nothing can keep it going. Everyone will get lost and won't even be able to see where they are. How can we not be sad?

Now then, for all the methods of the various schools, including the meditations and concentrations, liberations, insights, powers of elocution, seeing nature, realizing enlightenment, and all essential processes, there are scriptures and treatises, histories and writings, that clearly explain them. Even without actual transmission you can understand them on your own and attain them on your own. But when it comes to the transcendental bit of our Zen school, without learning from a teacher you can't master its subtleties.

How sad! Once Zen dies out, all Buddhism in the land will collapse.

Heaven and earth may be wide, but there is no other sun or moon. The rise or ruin of a nation depends on the leaders. Now if Buddhism declines and dies, the way of secular leadership will also be in danger. As I see Buddhism in the present time, nobody attains the Way. They just act as protectors of the nation, insofar as such virtues as they have all create blessings. When Buddhism is corrupted, and it is hard to learn the authentic Dharma, everyone puts forth their own opinions, and controversies rage.

For example, those who keep precepts and practice asceticism, mistakenly seeing merit, often experience human or celestial bliss thereby. Those who recite the name of a Buddha craving pleasure are therefore born in prosperous families. There are celestial pure lands; there are pure lands of ghost and spirit beings; there are pure lands of all tribes and communities. Those who seek rebirth wrongly, not relying on the right road, mostly don't get beyond these.

The Shingon, Tendai, and other paths of sages have no pre-eminent adepts or enlightened teachers,[3] so they just stick to the written word and do not look into the meaning of the scriptures. Instead, contention, conflict, egoism, and ignorance increase activities that lead to hell. Even if there are genuine practitioners, they still don't get out of aberrant views.

When it comes to our Zen school, you can't find a single individual who's genuinely right. Everyone falls into the views of the two vehicles or outsiders,[4] yet without being aware or cognizant of it themselves.

So learned gentlemen each study the ideas of their own sects to guide people; compared to their confused teaching, it would be better if there were no teaching at all. Why? It's one thing to be mistaken yourself; but you might lead any number of innocent people into false ways. That is truly lamentable!

At present I cannot avoid talking in these terms simply because I fear the collapse of Buddhism and the extinction of the sun of wisdom. That is why I am forced to draw distinctions, to convey this information to all people. Our true teaching does not make an issue of whether one is a monk or a layperson, a male or a female; it does not choose between the aristocrat and the commoner or the old and the young. It's not a question of great or small faculties, or of being smart or slow. As long as they have a great heart, ultimately none fail to succeed.

So believe deeply in this Dharma and urgently seek liberation. Set out as best you can; don't talk about the distance of the journey. The *Combined Treatise on the Flower Ornament* says,

To whom is the teaching of this scripture entrusted? This scripture's teaching is entrusted to ordinary people with great hearts.

---

3. "Paths of sages" is a term used in Pure Land Buddhism to refer to other types of Buddhism.

4. That is, either some sort of quietism, nihilism, or devotion to meditation states as ends in themselves.

The scripture says, "The teaching of this scripture does not come into the hands of other people." To interpret, "other people" means the three vehicles and outsiders who are attached to human or celestial conditions, as well as those who seek transcendental bliss. Why? This scripture does not admit bodhisattvas of the three vehicles; even with the six spiritual powers they still cannot hear the scripture and develop faith; how much the less the two vehicles and outsiders on human and celestial paths!

The scripture says, "Only true offspring of the King of Dharma, born in the family of those who arrive at reality, that is to say, ordinary people with great hearts, are able to believe and realize it." "Born in the family of those who arrive at reality" does not mean the great bodhisattvas already born in the family of Buddha. The Dharma is always expounded to living beings: if there are no greathearted ordinary people to believe and realize it, then this is not called entrusting, and not called circulation, because there is no one believing and no one attaining enlightenment. The scripture says, "But for these offspring, this scripture would perish." Were it not so, why would Buddha be concerned about this scripture perishing when the great bodhisattvas already born in the family of Buddha are already as numerous as atoms in infinite oceans of buddha worlds? Since he is not thinking about the great bodhisattvas who have already been born in the family of Buddha, obviously he must be thinking of ordinary people who are greathearted; it's not for those who are already among the sages. So we should recognize that this scripture is entrusted to ordinary people with great hearts.

This truth of ours is also like this, entrusted to all ordinary people with great hearts. "A great heart" means the capacity to believe this teaching—this is called a great heart. As for those who do not believe this teaching, even if they have the six spiritual powers, radiate great light, and complete countless holy paths, they are, after all, still small-minded people. They cannot be born in the family of Buddha, so they cannot carry out the practices of bodhisattvas.

Therefore the scripture says,

> Children of Buddha, even if there are bodhisattvas who practice the six ways of transcendence for countless millions of aeons and cultivate the various elements of enlightenment, if they have never heard of this teaching of inconceivable great virtue of those who arrive at reality, or if they hear at some times but do not believe, do not understand, do not follow, and do not enter it, they cannot be called real, true bodhisattvas, because they cannot be born in the family of Buddha. If they get to hear this teaching of infinite, inconceivable, unhindered, unobstructed knowledge and insight of those who arrive at reality, and, having heard, believe in it, follow it, understand it, and enter into it, know that these people will be born in the family of those who arrive at reality, accord with all the states of those who arrive at reality, and embody all the principles of bodhisattvas.

What does it mean to be born in the family of those who arrive at reality? Differentiated refined practice after enlightenment is the father; the basic great knowledge of seeing nature is the mother: when a single thought of faith is conceived between them, one is already in the womb of arrival at reality. From here on it's not a question of whether the road is long or short; setting out and progressively practicing, studying as thoroughly as possible, is all the process of "pregnancy." When the time comes that the work is complete, this is called coming to term. The various states that appear at this time are signs that the baby is about to emerge from the womb. If students keep on seeking without fixation on states that appear, one day realization will take place. This is called birth in the family of those who arrive at reality.

It is like the case of a newborn prince, whose intellect and ability are not yet like those of his father, the king; but his essential characteristics and all the nobility of his lineage are no different from his father, the king. Even the intelligent and capable officials and ministers of state cannot but respect him. So it is with the true heirs of those who arrive at reality, the kings of Dharma; their knowledge, eloquence, liberation, and spiritual capacities may not be comparable to Buddha, but clearly they are endowed with the essential characteristics of the Buddhas. Clearly they are fully imbued with the traits of the Buddhas. The nature of their knowledge, the nature of their eloquence, the nature of their liberation, the great expedients and great radiance of spiritual powers, great kindness, and great compassion, are no different from the Buddhas. Even bodhisattvas and arhats with liberation and spiritual powers cannot but honor them. Isn't that a pleasure?

Those who in the meantime get confused by visionary states, and conceive various views, are like miscarriages; they can never develop the subtle body of Buddha, except those who return to the true teaching, believe and enter into it, cultivate and realize it.

What does it mean to undertake the practice of bodhisattvas? It means not stopping at seeing nature, but using the verbal teachings of Buddhas and Masters for a hundred refinements, a thousand temperings, passing through any number of impenetrable barriers, transmitting the Zen masters' bit of progressive transcendence, helping up the fallen way of truth, upholding this attainment for the universal benefit of the future, so that the sun of wisdom will not die out. This is called bodhisattva practice.

It is like a prince gradually learning practical wisdom and the use of power, to succeed to his father's throne and disseminate instructions that will bring security to the world. And he also makes his own heir competent to succeed to his position. And on and on, one succeeding to another, for the eternal benefit of the nation. If he does not do this, even with a royal lineage he is the same as a commoner and ultimately benefits no one. If Zen monks linger in the principle of seeing nature and do not undertake bodhisattva practice, even if they have realized enlightenment, what use can they make of it?

You people should know this for a fact; this is an established principle, about which there can ultimately be no doubt. So you can cultivate initiation and birth in the family of those who arrive at reality in this way. Even those whose power of faith is not yet sufficient and whose power on the path is not yet full, if they develop pure faith deeply on arriving here, all of them are already in the womb of arrival at reality. Once in the womb, is there any reason they won't be born? Excepting only the miscarriages who fall into false views in the process, the rest all become true progeny of the Buddhas and Zen masters. Therefore scripture says, "Even hearing without believing still becomes a seed of faith; how much the more conceiving deep-seated pure faith!"

Those who get the human body, compared to those who lose the human body, are as the dirt on a fingernail compared to the entire earth. Now that you have been fortunate enough to have a human body, which is so rare, why don't you listen to this true teaching? Again and again, because you don't fear birth and death and you don't understand cause and effect, you just pursue immediate objects endlessly, without thinking about what happens after physical existence. When you're seeking material wealth for your own benefit, in your terms, is it not because you fear being afflicted by hunger and cold? Why are you not afraid of the afflictions of retribution? When you employ all sorts of expedients, craving for a profitable living, in your terms, is it not that you love the pleasures of aristocrats? Why do you not seek the pleasure of liberation?

What a shame! All people, religious and secular, give up the root and pursue the branches. They have no dignity at all.

Some, under the compulsions of psychological afflictions, argue over the beautiful and the ugly, unrestrained in their behavior, with no limit to the evil they'll do, heedless of the fact that the afflictions only bamboozle body and mind.[5]

Some, under the compulsions of clothing and food, argue over the fine and the coarse, killing and stealing, with no limit to the

---

5. "Affliction" is a technical term for mental conditions, behaviors, or complexes that cause misery. While said to be innumerable, the six main afflictions as traditionally defined in Buddhist psychology are greed, hatred, pride, ignorance, indecisiveness, and inaccurate perception.

evil they'll do, heedless of the fact that gold and grain are only for supporting self and others.

Some, under the compulsion of power and position, argue over high and low, greedy and wrathful, with no limit to the evil they'll do, heedless of the fact that power and position are only for governing society as a whole.

Some, under the compulsion of literature, argue over right and wrong, proud and jealous, with no limit to the evil they'll do, heedless of the fact that literature is only for reviewing past and present.

Some, under the compulsion of scriptural doctrines, debate which are deep and which shallow, contentious and egotistical, with no limit to the evil they'll do, heedless of the fact that scriptural doctrines only illustrate enlightened qualities.

Some, under the compulsion of Zen, debate over deviation and orthodoxy, ensnared by views and deluded by doctrine, with no limit to the evil they'll do, heedless of the fact that Zen is only a matter of doubting sayings.

All of them fail to return to the root, because they mistakenly pursue present objects. Going on and on this way ultimately makes them fall into the states of hells, hungry ghosts, and animals. Cause and effect are evident, like shadow following form. But if your mind is straightforward, without deviousness, then what difficulty is there to Buddhism?

Therefore the *Heroic Progress Scripture* says,

Now if you wish to cultivate supreme enlightenment and really discover the nature of illumination, you should reply to my questions with a straightforward mind. All in the ten directions who arrive at reality leave birth and death by the same path, all by means of a straightforward mind. As long as mind and speech are straightforward, then all the way through the stages there is never any deviation.

It is just because students do not rely on the straightforward mind that they erroneously produce judgments and do not find out the deep meaning. This is why there are so many obstacles.

If they set out with a straightforward mind, attend teachers with a straightforward mind, read the verbal teachings of Buddhas and Masters with a straightforward mind, study Zen and work on the path with a straightforward mind, the ignorant practice while ignorant, the stubborn practice while stubborn, those with lesser faculties practice with lesser faculties, those with many illnesses practice with many illnesses, the young practice while young, the old practice while old, the poor and the rich and the noble and the common practice while poor or rich or noble or common, the busy practice while busy: What is so is considered so, what is not is considered not; success is considered success, failure is considered failure, attainment is considered attainment, not yet having attained is considered not yet having attained. Nothing is covered up. The terms *right* and *wrong* are not heard; the terms *gain* and *loss* are not heard. Those who have arrived are real in arrival; those who have not yet arrived are real in not having arrived. Thus knowledge and ignorance, affliction and enlightenment, are all real truth, all in accord with the true Dharma.

It's not a matter of stopping at this affirmation; the point is not to lose the opportunity to progress and discover enlightenment by this means, penetrating naturally without belaboring the mind.

Now I also have ten principles to indicate to students how to apply the mind. Please examine them thoroughly.

1. Vows of compassion—deep and serious
2. Willpower—above and beyond
3. Perceptive capacity—broad and great
4. The mirror of knowledge—high and clear
5. Seeing the Way—transcendent attainment
6. Practical application—lucid and sure
7. Human feelings—shut off
8. Worldly thoughts—let go
9. Repentance—intense
10. Doubt—thoroughgoing

Constantly test your own mind with these ten principles. If you can trust these principles and put them into practice, everything will be accomplished as easily as pointing to the palm of your hand.

The Buddhas of past, present, and future attain true enlightenment and initiate bodhisattvas by seeing nature alone, so you need to see nature first.

All living beings—bodhisattvas and disciples, people of all races and nations, all philosophies and religions, all occupational classes, all ages, religious and secular, male and female, eunuch and hermaphrodite, gigolo and harlot, the handicapped, incorrigibles, even other species, monsters and ghouls, ghosts, beasts, and denizens of hells, if they can believe in this teaching and can practice it, progressing as best they can, attaining realization as best they can, I now explicitly predict they will certainly attain buddhahood, whether in this life or the next.

Even if they believe but don't practice, it still becomes a seed of buddhahood; and in the future each and every one will become a Buddha. Even hearing without believing still creates powerful associations that will eventually produce deep-rooted pure faith in the true Dharma in the future.

Past bodhisattvas attained buddhahood by this means; present bodhisattvas attain buddhahood by this means; future bodhisattvas will attain buddhahood by this means. This is the straight and true highway of practice of all Buddhas.

At the time, a novice bodhisattva, hearing the teaching expounded in this *Undying Lamp*, was filled with doubt and confusion and came to ask questions.

QUESTION: Is seeing nature and realizing the Way really attaining buddhahood?

ANSWER: It is really attaining buddhahood.

QUESTION: The Buddhas all have spiritual powers and radiate lights. If you've already become a Buddha, Master, then why don't you have these?

ANSWER: I certainly do have spiritual powers and radiate lights.

QUESTION: Why don't you show them?

ANSWER: I'm always showing them; you yourself don't see. It's like a blind man's inability to see is not the fault of the sun and moon.

QUESTION: Even so, the Buddhas have used spiritual powers and radiated lights to awaken faith in people, manifesting various miracles. Why don't you do so?

ANSWER: There are greater spiritual powers and lesser spiritual powers;[6] there are greater lights and lesser lights. What I have attained are the great ones; what you're asking about are the lesser ones. The greater ones are the great functions manifested by basic perception of nature; the lesser ones are just offshoots, extra powers developed in the process of cultivation. Our school only points to the root and does not discuss the branches. When the root is fully developed, the outgrowths appear of themselves. If you want to have branches, foliage, flowers, and fruit without the root and trunk, that is impossible.

What is more, showing miracles deludes people and actually obscures basic nature. They all think, "He is a saint; this is beyond us," and wind up unable to believe in the spiritual powers and radiant lights inherent in themselves. For this reason the wise do not use extra powers even if they have them.

The thirty-two marks of distinction and eighty kinds of refinements, the supernatural powers, radiance, and so on, do not constitute the original body of Buddha; they are signs of excellence, borrowed temporarily to induce admiration in people of lesser faculties. Therefore universal rulers have the thirty-two marks of distinction, while devotees of various deities have supernatural powers and radiance. Even titans, spiritual immortals, powerful ghouls, and foxes and badgers with the power of concentration all perform these magical projections, producing all sorts of appearances.

By way of analogy, even the water held in cupped hands will reflect things if it's still, whereas the vast ocean makes no reflec-

---

6. For the bases of spiritual powers in a One Vehicle context, see *The Flower Ornament Scripture*, p. 730.

tions when in movement. Generally speaking, magical projections all come from concentration power. Arhats have spiritual capacities and bodhisattvas have spiritual powers because the lesser vehicles emphasize cultivation of concentration power, so spiritual capacities are easily awakened. The Great Vehicle cultivates comprehensive knowledge and expedients, so concentration power is hard to perfect. Great vessels take a long time to complete, but once their capacities are mature, they are therefore beyond the scope of other vehicles, which lose their shine like a lone lamp under the sun.

It is like plants and trees, which sprout only when the most mature and well-developed fruits are taken and buried in the earth. Then the cause does not differ from the result, and the result does not differ from the cause. If a cause is at variance with the result, that is not the real cause; if a result is at variance with the cause, that result is random. You just discuss result upon result while remaining at cause within cause; since even the cause is not completed, how could the result be?

Our school directly distinguishes result within cause and cultivates cause upon result. Since the cause is thus, how could the result not be so? Please try to consider this in terms of the seeding of plants and trees.

As for bodhisattvas of lesser vehicles who occasionally manifest spiritual powers and demonstrate miracles, because they enjoy the lesser teachings and attain lesser results, because they rely on the power of lesser concentration and release lesser spiritual powers, because they exert a lesser educational influence by less-impressive virtues, they cannot attain the great result, cannot fathom the knowledge of Buddhas, cannot instruct people with greater faculties, and cannot circulate the teachings of the Supreme Vehicle.

All of them are lesser in faculties, lesser in knowledge, lesser in will and action, mistakenly ignoring the fundamental and pursuing the trivial. Even if they manage to develop spiritual capacities, radiance, and innumerable phenomena on the Way, because these are not perception of nature, they are not real Buddhism, since they are not teachings manifested by one's own nature. So if you want to attain spiritual capacities and radiance, first you have to see nature.

As an analogy, it is like the way a good doctor first treats the internal and then treats the external. If you treat the external first and don't treat the internal, because the root of the illness has not been extracted, even if the treatment has extraordinary effect, the illness will eventually recur.

It should be realized that treating external maladies always has quick results, while treating internal maladies not only has no immediate results, but also activates and spreads hidden maladies, so external maladies flare up even more. This is why the ignorant first crave quick results and value treatment of external illnesses. For this reason they have many illnesses over the years without ever being able to penetrate the way to real health without illness.

When the root of disease is deep, then it is necessary to use potent medicine. When an illness is slight, then a single packet of medicine can cure it. So, as the inborn nature of people of high antiquity was full and substantial, they generally had no illnesses; and even if they got sick, they didn't need a lot of medicine. Since middle antiquity, people's faculties have been insubstantial and weak; as soon as they get sick, they use potent medicines, or seek various curative methods, before they can extirpate the root of the illness.

So it is with Buddhism. The ancients were innocent and sincere people, so they could be treated with middling and lesser methods. The present time is different; everyone has deep-rooted illnesses, so but for the medicines of the One Vehicle—seeing nature, differentiation, merging, function, and progressive transcendence—even if the external seems cured, the internal will never be cured.

Worldly people say that the path of sages existed in the era of the true Dharma, but in the imitative and terminal eras there is no practice or realization at all. How stupid! If you said that even though an illness is severe there's no need for potent medicine, would that be logical? If you discuss the difficulty or ease of practice and realization, it is not only the teaching of the Higher

Vehicle, but also the teachings of the Middle and Lower Vehicles too, that are hard to practice and realize.

On the whole, difficulty and ease are in the person, not the teaching. It's like medicine—whether or not it is taken is the responsibility of the person, not the medicine. Those who think middling and lesser teachings are effective because they're easy to practice and realize are just treating external ailments with quick cures, not getting genuine effects.

The formulas they sell in common drugstores are inexpensive, yet the effects they claim are still quite remarkable. Even so, when it comes to curing chronic illness, do you think they'll work? It is necessary to use the marvels of potent medicines and hygienic techniques to cure this. Why would anyone think Buddhism alone is otherwise?

As for the statement that there is no practice or realization in the imitative and terminal eras, this is just something Buddha said out of pity for people of the terminal era who do not believe in the true teaching.[7] It's like saying that the mental and physical illnesses of the last age are so deep-seated that few get cured even if they take medicines. While this is so, if you willingly stay sick and don't take potent medicine, madness and disease will intensify, until you can no longer get up.

Leaving aside for the moment the mad not knowing they're mad, if you know you're sick, you cannot but take medicine. Knowing you're sick, first seek potent medicine.

As for the mad nowadays, they only believe the words of the mad and do not believe the instructions of the sane. They can only be pitied.

Sickness of the physical body, however serious, does not, after all, go beyond this life. Sickness of the spiritual body stays in a toxic sea since beginningless time, inspired by six

---

7. This refers to the concept of three periods of a teaching—genuine, imitation, and terminal. A genuine teaching meets the needs of its time; an imitation teaching mimics in hopes it will work; a terminal teaching is a token. According to the *Scripture of the Great Demise*, the defining characteristic of the last age, or the terminal era, is when the teaching is sold in pieces like a commodity.

bandits, enslaved by five desires.[8] The fever of anger and the humidity of craving get into the bones and penetrate the marrow, extremely hard to heal. How can ordinary medicine cure this? You need to find the medicine that is really right before you'll succeed.

Some say the root of disease is so deep it cannot be cured by one's own effort, and requires a journey to the realm of the Expert Physician of the West to cure it.[9] This is also a temporary expedient. It is like coaxing children who know no better and won't take medicine, appealing to their likes to induce them to take medicine. Scripture says, "In the buddha lands of the ten directions there is only the teaching of One Vehicle; there is no second or third, except as expedient doctrines of Buddha, just using terms to induce and lead people."[10] So what the Good Doctor of the West gives is also the wonder drug of the One Vehicle. Since that and this are equally methods of the One Vehicle, why bother to go elsewhere?[11]

The Buddha saw the insane were not taking medicine, so in his great compassion he devised expedients, first concentrating medicines in the four truths and twelve causes and conditions, and getting them to imbibe these.[12] Then he concentrated medi-

---

8. "Six bandits" refers to the six major afflictions, noted above. "Five desires" refers to the five elemental senses, as the doorways of desire.

9. This refers to the doctrine of *tariki*, or other-power, of Pure Land Buddhism. The "Expert Physician" is Amitabha, the Buddha of Infinite Light, who is also called Amitayur, the Buddha of Infinite Life; the Pure Land, Sukhavati, or Blissful, is said to be in the West, the direction of the setting sun, in Zen taken to symbolize the cessation of thoughts.

10. This is a famous line of the *Lotus-sutra*, introducing the Ekayana or One Vehicle.

11. Hakuin used to say that people who succeeded in Pure Land practice turned to Zen, while people who failed at Zen turned to Pure Land practice. The Zen meaning of "elsewhere" here is not that people shouldn't study other schools, as indeed this treatise insists that Zen students should study all schools; rather it is a reminder that otherworldly visionary experiences induced by Pure Land methods are not goals in themselves.

12. For a One Vehicle view of "the four truths", see "The Four Holy Truths," book 8 of *The Flower Ornament Scripture,* and stages three and four of "The

cines in the six perfections and recommended these.[13] For Lady Vaidehi he concentrated medicines in sixteen visualizations,[14] while for people of lesser potential he secreted medicine in rebirth by invocation of Amida Buddha.[15]

With this, the insane gradually got a taste for them and took the medicines that suited them, each seeing its effect. Now, seeing the insane gradually revert to sanity, in the Universal teachings he turned around and criticized those medicines as inferior and said these were therefore not real substantial effects; and he praised the effects of the real medicines specially taken by the bodhisattvas.

When the patients heard of these, they all wanted some, but because they were attached to their previous tastes, after all it was hard to give them up. That is why he added the Dharma medicine of insight, infusing them all equally. Unawares, the patients became increasingly sane, each seeing the effect of real medicine.

Even so, this was still no more than expedient method; but because they got addicted to substitute medicine and didn't seek real medicine, he established methods based on the principle of emptiness.

Ten Stages," book 26, pp. 721–35. For "the twelve causes and conditions," see stage six of "The Ten Stages" in book 26 of *The Flower Ornament Scripture,* pp. 745–49.

13. The first six of ten perfections or ways of transcendence; see *Buddhist Yoga,* chapter 7, "The Transcendent Ways of the Stages."

14. This refers to the scripture on the visualization of the Buddha of Infinite Life, one of the main texts of Pure Land Buddhism. Lady Vaidehi is the figure who receives this teaching in a dream vision while she is imprisoned and unable to meet the Buddha in person.

15. "Amida" is the Japanese rendering of Amitabha, the visionary Buddha of Infinite Light, also taken to refer to mind itself. This Buddha is the main object of devotion of Pure Land schools. According to the most popular versions of Japanese Pure Land Buddhism, people immersed in ordinary life generally can't perfect the sixteen visualizations of Infinite Life, and that is why for them the so-called Special Vow of Amida Buddha provides that even those who simply recite the name of the Buddha will be reborn in that Buddha's pure land. Munan called this practice a sharp sword to cut off random thoughts; in Zen it is understood as an expedient to purify the mind, but it is also combined with the introspection of *who* is doing it.

Later, at the Lotus assembly, he set aside all expedients and administered to all alike the medicine of complete, all-at-once, subtle perception of nature's real characteristics. The people became very joyful, now realizing they had hitherto been taking substitute medicine in error. From now on, with the Dharma medicine of the ghee of nirvana, he extirpated the roots of all illnesses everywhere,[16] so they would be physically and mentally healthy and ultimately reach the realm of great comfort where there is no illness and fully develop the ability to act independently without hindrance. This is called the Flower Ornament universe. The aspect of finishing tasks and returning to repose, abiding stably in self-mastery, is called the mystery of the Mantra. These two scriptures both belong to the Vehicle of Mystic Projection, so they are not verbal teachings of the Buddha.[17]

This is called the completion of the tasks of the King of Physicians.[18] Now tell me, what about our final bit of transcendence outside of doctrine? What does it illuminate? When you get here, please be equipped with another eye.

So students of our school have the times of the Buddha's lifetime of teachings in themselves. When they first hear the verbal teachings of Buddhas and Masters, they are as if deaf and mute, as in the Flower Ornament assembly. Doing Zen meditation, they first understand the principle of emptiness and develop various views, mistaking this for the ultimate. This is like the attainments of the three vehicles of the Agamas. Then, calling them visionary states, repudiating them and taking them away, seeking true realization beyond, corresponds to the Universal scriptures. Spurring on determination further, not choosing among

16. This does not refer to the tranquil nirvana of the lesser vehicles, but to buddha-nature; here "nirvana" alludes to the *Mahaparinirvana-sutra*, in which buddha-nature is symbolized by ghee, clarified butter being the most quintessential and refined realization of the potential in milk.

17. The Shingon or Mantra school is based on two Vajrayana texts, the *Mahavairocana-sutra* and the *Vajrasekhara-sutra*. Esoteric Vajrayana texts are represented as mystically projected.

18. An epithet of Buddha. "The completion of tasks" refers to the cycle of teachings of his lifetime.

views but deeply seeking the source of attainments, is equivalent to the great sutra on perfection of insight. When the time comes and efforts ripen, it appears without being sought, like the *Lotus-sutra*'s teaching of One Vehicle. Also finding out the principle of essential nature as clearly as seeing it in the palm of the hand is just like the *Nirvana-sutra*. Clearly comprehending and successfully penetrating the differentiating statements of Buddhas and Masters is like returning to the Flower Ornament universe. When their state is peaceful, within it's like entering the Mystic Array. Finally, progressively transcending, having a life beyond, is the experience of our school, communicated outside of doctrine. Isn't this great?

Recently, Pure Land Buddhists who have yet to find out the import of the school blindly claim the path of sages is hard to practice and therefore ineffective. They say only remembrance of Buddha is easy to practice and therefore of superior worth. Ho hum. Remembrance of Buddha? This is an esoteric expedient of the Buddhas. Buddha provisionally set up this teaching for a segment of lesser abilities; if he told them about the real vehicle immediately, because of the weakness of their power of faith, their minds would not be focused and they could not perfect absorption and form a deep affinity with it. By emphasizing the power of Buddha for the time being, faith has something to rely on, so absorption is easily developed. Therefore those who simply believe in remembrancing Buddha are assuredly reborn. When they keep up remembrance without concern with affirmation or negation, without mixing in random thoughts, then total absorption will suddenly occur; this is called rebirth.

When Amida Buddha's marks of distinction and refinements, radiant lights, and all teachings appear before your eyes, the Land of Bliss, with its arrays of positive qualities and all its outstanding features, fills heaven and earth; every single thought is the Seer of the Sound of the World, the individual in action is the Greatly Empowered One;[19] music of twenty-five types fills

---

19. "Seer of the Sound of the World" is one way the name of the supernal bodhisattva Avalokitesvara was translated. The "Greatly Empowered One" refers

the ears, food and clothing of eighty-four thousand kinds are provided at every seat; rivers, birds, and woods all remembrance the Buddha, the Dharma, and the Community; and the mountains, rivers, and earth fully reveal the subtle functions of knowledge of principle and phenomena; this is called realization of the highest class of rebirth in the present life.

As for those whose faith is not complete, because of the power of remembrancing Buddha, they'll be born in an expedient buddha land. This is called future rebirth. However, it is not beyond the level of middle or lower grades.

As for those who strive for the higher grades of rebirth and practice progressively as best they can, because their effort is on the cause of understanding, they also attain the highest results. Though born in a buddha land and having become princes of Dharma along with the likes of Manjusri, Samantabhadra, Avalokitesvara, and Mahasthamaprapta, they are content to be lowly, inferior people. As for those who only crave rebirth, their effort is on causal conditions, so they will attain results of lesser vehicles. Even in buddha lands they will still be listeners, solitary illuminates, or lesser-vehicle bodhisattvas.

As an analogy, suppose there is a country in the East called Tsune and a country in the West called Nori. Now the country of Tsune is in chaos, a military emergency. The king of Tsune, therefore, pitying the people, announces to everyone, "Our country is in turmoil, not fit for ordinary people to live in. Now the king of the country of Nori has great kindness and compassion, and is able to support destitute people. You should hasten to that land; the king of Nori will surely show you mercy, and you will have plenty of food and clothing."

Now the destitute who lack firm will all encourage their families to seek to reach that country. That country is far away, beyond a hundred thousand million mountains and seas, so many of them have trouble, and not a few of them die. Only a few

---

to the supernal bodhisattva Mahasthamaprapta. These two bodhisattvas are envisioned as the main assistants of Amitabha (Amida) Buddha in the Land of Bliss.

among them, those who have the strength of deep faith and those who have gotten aboard the sturdy ship of great vows, ultimately avoid all those hardships. As soon as they reach the other shore, the king of Nori, moved with tremendous pity, gives them all goods and valuables, providing everyone with fields and houses, enabling them to enjoy peace, prosperity, and pleasure forever.

As for the inhabitants of the country of Tsune who have spunk, they say to one another, "Though our country is in turmoil, we're not without our leader; why should we emulate the ambition of common men to go to the trouble of getting welfare from another leader? We would rather leave our corpses lying at the gates of the citadel than ever trade the path of humanity and justice for personal gain. We should exert our utmost efforts to revive the nation." With this, they raise an army and launch a righteous war, destroying the enemy's fortresses, killing treasonous ministers, rectifying injustices, and caring for the common people. Then the king of Tsune, greatly pleased, has rewards for everyone.

Thus for the knights of justice and principle are the honors of the highest offices and the emoluments of kings and lords; how could their nobility and glory be equaled by the people of Nori? Even the king of Nori, hearing his name, says, "The king of Tsune has an abundance of loyal subjects, which I cannot equal," and envies him from afar. If he comes for a visit, it is with a great show of respect and reverent offerings of all sorts of delicacies.

It is also like the case of people in the world who have rather strong will; they can prosper by running their own business, whereas the unreliable give up their own professions and become dependents of rich houses, barely keeping themselves alive. Everyone originally has the nature of a Buddha; everyone is a member of the royal family of Dharma and an heir to a tycoon. How can they be born in that family and yet disavow its character for themselves? How sad! It may be understandable in the intractable and base-minded who have no wisdom and utterly no affinity with good, but what about those with some spunk who know right from wrong—how can they have no concern about this?

Saint Honen said in the Ohara debate,[20] "Ultimate Bliss is not far:[21] It is made out to be ten myriad million lands West. Amida is in your own mind, manifesting a form on a lotus seat." He also said, "It should be realized that self-power and other-power mean the same as strength and weakness." Also, "Although there are strong and weak, both are the power of reality." Also, "Going from formal practice as cause, entering right into formless bliss as result, restrains the notion of rebirth and enables realization of the unborn noumenon." Also, "'Rebirth' is no birth."

These points merit serious reflection.

On Diamond Discipline [by the same author] says, "'Diamond discipline' means the inherent nature of mind is the substance of the discipline of the Great Vehicle. The substance of discipline in general is the mind of living beings."

Also, "Why do you seek the realm of Buddha outside your own mind?"

Also, "To begin with, the words remembrancing Buddha should be understood. As for remembrance, having no thoughts is called remembrance. As for Buddha, the buddha of mind is called Buddha."

Also, "In general terms, Ultimate Bliss is a different name for form, but there is still no form to see; Amida is a different name for mind, but where is there mind to be found? So Ultimate Bliss and Amida are really not external objects, but are in your own mind. Scripture says, 'It's not far from here. . . . This mind is Buddha.'"

Surely Honen was really not a bodhisattva of a temporary vehicle; he must have been a great bodhisattva of the complete, all-at-once inconceivable, who deeply pitied people of the terminal era lost in illusion and temporarily manifested embodiment to come liberate strong people. Now when it comes to the One Ve-

20. Honen (1133-1212) is revered as the founder of the Japanese Pure Land school called Jodo Shu. Several Pure Land schools branched off from the Jodo Shu, including the Jodo Shin Shu, or Shinshu for short, the largest of all Japanese Buddhist sects, founded by Honen's disciple Shinran (1173-1262).

21. "Ultimate Bliss" is the Chinese translation of the Sanskrit Sukhavati, "Blissful," which is the name of Amida Buddha's pure land.

hicle teaching of seeing nature, those without great Zen masters who've already attained, invariably fall into views of outsiders or the two vehicles, and many commit the sin of slandering truth.

Those who can hear true teaching and attain the way to it transcend everything and immediately ascend to the state of buddhahood. Those who meet false teachers and believe false understandings fall into wrong views, with no hope of ever getting out.

There is benefit and there is harm. There is that which should be honored and that which should be feared. So an era with enlightened guides has abundant benefits, but when there are no teachers, without expedients like this, how could people sunk in confusion be able to form better conditions?[22]

People of the era of imitation, in conformity with mediocre and lesser minds, are basically humble and reverential, so even if they develop divergent views they don't become antisocial.[23] With the sole exception of those guilty of repudiating the Great Vehicle, everyone else can create conditions for seeing Buddha. That is why there is benefit for mediocre and lesser people.

It's like a standard remedy, which may not be worth using when you have a good doctor available, but does have some benefit when there's no doctor. Even so, because a standard remedy has a fixed formula, it is hard for the effect to be thorough. It is not as good as a skilled physician with deep knowledge of the root of illnesses who adjusts the medicine for the specific illness.

This is why our school does not take names or forms but first realizes the mind of Buddha and then the doctrines of Buddha. The teachings he set up may seem contradictory, but their uses of accommodation and opposition all accord with Buddha's intent. I only pray that those who practice remembrance of Buddha will do their best to ascend to the higher stage, where you forget

22. This refers to the Pure Land expedient, which contains its own prescription.

23. That is, they imitate out of respect, so even though they aren't enlightened, they are not entirely unrestrained.

the notion of rebirth and experience the nonbeing of self-existence. You should find out the inner meaning of remembrancing Buddha, to liberate everyone in the future.

Generally speaking, all the schools, hard to practice and easy to practice, have two principles in common. In the context of expedients, remembrancing Buddha is considered easy to practice, when the mind cannot concentrate on the other practices. In the context of the real vehicles, seeing nature is considered easy practice, as all Buddha's teachings emerge from this.

The Three Treatises are based on real emptiness. Real emptiness is fundamental knowledge of essential nature. Therefore you must turn to your own mind to clarify fundamental knowledge. Once the fundamental is clear, distinctions become self-evident, like images of objects all appearing in a mirror when it's clear. Use this to see the eighty thousand sacred doctrines of the treasury of all teachings—the Hosso, Tendai, Kegon, and Shingon; then you know them without having learned them, attain them without having cultivated them. Is this not a way of easy practice?

If you pursue the written word, chasing branches and leaves, in order to clarify the meanings of the schools, your physical faculties are limited, whereas the treasuries of teachings are inexhaustible. Even if you labored for immense aeons, you could not comprehend the path of the subtle mysteries of the Three Treatises.

Hosso [Characteristics of Phenomena] is based on subtle existence.[24] Subtle existence means subtle knowledge of differentiation. First turn to your own nature to clarify knowledge of differentiation, and fundamental knowledge naturally cannot but appear. Use this subtle mirror to see the other teachings and the transcendental key of the school, as well as the forms of adaptive practice, are attained at once, with complete clarity. Wouldn't that be pleasant?

Tendai is based on the unique character of reality of the middle

---

24. For the *Sandhinirmocana-sutra,* one of the two main scriptural sources of Hosso, see *Buddhist Yoga.*

way, considering the two principles of real emptiness and subtle existence to be individually one-sided.[25] The character of reality is the totality inherent in our own nature. Therefore, thoroughly clarify your own nature and you transcend the nominal boundary between real emptiness and subtle existence, and the untainted subtle knowledge of the character of reality will naturally appear. Because it completely comprehends everything, it is called round, or complete; because it attains all at once, it is called sudden, or all-at-once. If you see everything with this subtle knowledge, what reason could there be for failing to comprehend?

The Kegon [Flower Ornament] is based on the realm of reality.[26] The realm of reality is like where the hundred rivers return to the ocean and lose all their names, equally becoming water of the ocean. In the Kegon teaching, there is nothing else, so samsara and nirvana, afflictions and enlightenment, each atom, each blade of grass, fills the substance of reality, so principle and phenomena interpenetrate, and phenomena interpenetrate, and nature and characteristics merge. This is called the realm of reality.

Pointing to where the mind-flower opens up is called the Lotus of the True Teaching [Hokke]; pointing to where the mind-flower fully blooms is called the Flower Ornament [Kegon]. The Lotus of the True Teaching and the Flower Ornament are one and the same principle and substance; their only difference is of order. Therefore both scriptures are originally included in the Tendai teaching. First you find out the meaning of the character of reality of seeing nature; once you enter the inner sanctum, then the Flower Ornament reality-realm naturally becomes clear. If you know and see in this way, would there be any teaching you didn't attain? There would only be more, that's all.[27]

Shingon is based on the fundamental uncreated. The Hokke and Kegon both teach instantaneous relative origination, so since relative origination has no beginning, it is called fundamentally

25. On Tendai meditation, see *Stopping and Seeing*.

26. On Kegon meditation, see *Entry into the Realm of Reality*.

27. This refers to the endless infinitude of the realm of reality, pervaded by the same principles.

uncreated. The simple fact of noncreation, however, contains infinite teachings, so all the teachings are esoteric. As soon as you get into verbal discussion, it all falls into exoteric principles; so again, to communicate the nature of reality beyond verbal explanation, esoteric symbols may be shown.

Also, the diamond element is the knowledge of the fundamental uncreated; the womb element is the principle of the fundamental uncreated.[28] Real knowledge is firm and solid, so it is called diamond. Real principle is pregnant, so it is called a womb. Whenever principle is spoken of, it is the same as the exoteric scriptures, but when speaking of the principles inherent in the substance of the uncreated, they are all called esoteric for that reason.

Whenever there's any speech, that's not the body of reality. To nevertheless consider the body of reality to be the teacher [in Shingon], points to the reality inherent in that uncreated substance. Therefore it is called the reality-body expounding the teaching. This teaching only began in the second five centuries [after Buddha's death], in the time of Nagarjuna,[29] because esoteric teaching was not needed in the age of purity of the true teaching; they were able to understand the esoteric principles spontaneously. But when the sun of true teaching set, people's faculties gradually declined and many got stuck on exoteric principles, so that's how this [esoteric] teaching got started. This belongs to the Buddha's inconceivable treasury of empowerment by spiritual projection; it alone goes beyond the forty-nine years

28. The main mandalas containing the Shingon teachings are called the *vajra*, or diamond, mandala and the womb mandala, or the diamond and womb realms of reality. The diamond generally corresponds to the phenomenal, the womb to the noumenal.

29. The eras of the true teaching and imitation teaching are said to have lasted five hundred years each, while the terminal age is supposed to last for ten thousand years. It is not really known when Nagarjuna lived, but some place him in the first century B.C.E., some in the first century C.E. He is considered a virtual second Buddha, a patriarch of Tantric Shingon Buddhism as well as Zen, Three Treatise, Tendai, and Pure Land schools. See *The Ecstasy of Enlightenment* for the roles of emptiness, mind, and self-realization in the so-called *sahaja* or "natural" school of esoteric Buddhism.

[of Buddha's teaching]. It is like when Bodhidharma arrived [in China] everyone had fallen into dogma, so he simply established a separate practice outside doctrine, not depending on scriptures or treatises. All of this was adaptation to the time and response to potential—there's never been a fixed teaching.

It is like the case of a skilled physician who does not keep one formula in mind but prescribes various formulas, according to the illnesses. Thus there are fundamentally no two teachings in Buddhism. Those who can find the intent of a school will not fail to attain any of them, will not fail to master any of them.

If we were to impose labels and ranks on them, then keeping precepts, asceticism, all constructed roots of good, are like originating in an isolated village with nothing to foster concentration or insight. Also, when you get lost in the wilds, as long as you have food and clothing you enjoy sightseeing, but when your provisions are exhausted you suffer hunger and cold; the finest rewards of human and celestial states do not go beyond this.

Meditation, concentration, knowledge, and insight are like progressing along a road; without vows of compassion, you'll stop at an inn, managing a day's rent, remaining poor and lowly forever. The psychic powers of disciples, individual illuminates, celestials, and outsiders are the results. Lesser-vehicle bodhisattvas may have vows of compassion, but their will is weak and they don't find out the whole route. It is like going into the house of a territorial official; though he has nobility, it is not yet truly real. To have the spunk to go beyond these stages and find out the whole route is like gazing upon the royal capital.

The meanings of the Great Vehicle schools are all experiences in the royal capital, so the Sanron [Three Treatises] is like the gateway of the citadel, the Hosso [Characteristics of Phenomena] is like the center of the citadel, the Hokke [Lotus of the True Teaching] is like the palace gate, the Kegon [Flower Ornament] is like the audience hall, the Shingon [Mantra] is like the treasury. So, for the principles of all teachings, and the results obtained in the environment and in the people, the Kegon is considered clear and comprehensive, as it shows magnificent arrays in the hall. For all valuable resources and the abode of the Buddhas, Shingon is considered right, because when tasks are done, everything is returned to storage.

And when it comes to entry, the Hokke is considered foremost, because if it is indeed the gate to the palace you naturally go through it, whereas if you mistake the gate you'll enter someone else's house. As for the teaching that is entered into, the esoteric is foremost, because the ruler and all precious implements are in the treasury, as things are accomplished in the exoteric realm and concealed in the esoteric.

Even so, when you reach the meanings of the schools, there is no difference at all. It's like people seeking the abode of the emperor; first the gate of the citadel is pointed out to them, and the wise go all the way into the citadel and don't stop until they meet the emperor. Those lacking knowledge, in contrast, don't know the distinction, so they wind up stopping as soon as they reach the gateway to the citadel.

Overall, though there are nominal distinctions in the causal stage, when you reach the resulting realization there is no difference. It is like the hundred rivers have differences but the ocean does not. All the streams of the teaching lead to the ocean of fundamental nature, whereat they equally become knowledge-water of uniform flavor.

All living beings in the world depend on the ocean, so the Sanron and Hosso should not fail to penetrate the Tendai and Shingon, and the Tendai and Shingon should not fail to go through the Sanron and Hosso. The same goes for all the other teachings.

Just beware of all streams of the teaching flowing outward and thus never being able to enter the ocean of the fundamental all-knowledge of the Buddhas. Confucianism, Taoism, and Shinto were all taught according to conditions by bodhisattvas in the stage equivalent to enlightenment who concealed their virtues, hid their light, and appeared to be like other people. These naturally help the teaching of the One Vehicle of seeing nature inwardly, while providing perennial guidelines for society outwardly. Mundane people think they're mutually exclusive because their doctrines differ and their terms are distinct, so they each conceive views of "them" and "us," not only doing injury to Buddhism but also obscuring those doctrines, making them worse than the ignorant. How sad!

Sages devised doctrines differently to adapt to the times, but they just wanted people to follow them back to the root. People of high antiquity originally had straightforward minds, so as soon as they heard directions they got right to the source. Even if the instructions were crude, their effect was more than enough. People of the last age lost the substantiality of original nature; seeking vanities in their insubstantiality, they destroyed the truth in its substance. Therefore Buddhism is very detailed and precise, and even so educates and reforms with difficulty— how much the more Confucianism, Taoism, and Shinto![30]

Thus the *Basic Record Constituting the Supremely Secret Treasure of the Shrine* says,[31]

In the winter of the twenty-sixth year of the reign of Ikume Irihiko Isachi no Mikoto,[32] on the night of the ceremony of testing the new crops in the eleventh lunar month, eighty priests and priestesses attended the announcement: "Tonight I have received a revelation of an awesome command of the great spirit." (Yamato-hime no Mikoto received and announced the revelation of the great spirit.)[33] The priests and priestesses were attentive, undistracted, hearing it accurately

30. This comment refers to the times; the comparison of religions is not made in terms of superiority but complexity. The idea is that the more the times deteriorate, the more "medicines" are needed, but even though Buddhism has a larger inventory of expedients than the other ways as generally known, it is still proving hard to produce the desired effects.

31. "The Shrine" refers to the Shinto shrine at Ise, associated with the imperial house.

32. This is the name of Emperor Suinin, who is supposed to have been the tenth emperor, reigning from 29 B.C.E. to 70 C.E. Ancient tombs are not accessible to shed light on the historicity of this emperor.

33. This is parenthetical in the original. The other parenthetical notes relate Shinto to Buddhism and Confucianism. The medium, whose name means "Princess of Yamato," was the fourth daughter of Emperor Suinin. Yamato was the name of the ancient state that came to rule Japan and so is also used as a literary name for Japan.

and clearly. "Humans are the spiritual beings of the earth (self-help); they should take responsibility for tranquility and peace (aspiration). The mind is the host of the spirits (helping others). Don't hurt the spirit in the mind (courtesy)."

The Spirit Vehicle [Shinto] puts prayer first; unseen assistance is based on honesty. (Necessarily.) When everyone is enabled to attain the Great Way by their original commitments,[34] then the world is harmonious, the sun and moon are clear, wind and rain are in season, the country is prosperous, and the people are secure.

Therefore spiritual people kept the primitive and excluded any breath of Buddhism. In general, in the spirit age, people's hearts were wise and constant, honest and upright. As for the descendants of the earth spirits, such as the ordinary people everywhere in the world, the spirits in their minds are dark; they divide different terms of existence and nonexistence; their minds race compulsively, with never a time of rest. Their hearts break and their spirits scatter; when their spirits scatter, their bodies die.

Humans are endowed with the ethereal energies of heaven and earth; if they do not respect what the ethereal energies produce, seeing the light-progeny of the spirits, because they don't believe in the taboos of the spirits, they submerge in the darkness of the long night of birth and death, and sigh in the underworld. Because of this, the realized human of the West, in place of the imperial divinity, instructed assiduously, teaching people to cultivate good, giving out teachings according to capacities. Since then the great spirit has returned to the original position.

Ah, it truly is so: In the innocent age of high antiquity, people's minds were upright and honest and could easily attain the Great Way according to their faculties and capacities. Since spirit people

---

34. That is to say, by their own religion. Although this is represented as a revelation of ancient times, it was written after Confucianism, Taoism, and Buddhism were already in Japan.

kept the primitive, what need had they for news of Buddhism? Then, as the last age eventually arrived, they lost their original mind and ran seeking outside, pursuing objects in their confusion, thus whirled about in birth and death, sinking and suffering in miserable states. At this point, if not for the Buddha's subtle teaching, how could they get free of birth and death?

It also says, "Shinto emerges from the borders of the primeval and returns to the origin of the primeval. The Three Treasures[35] refute views of existence and nonexistence to realize the ground of the character of reality. This is the highest ultimate message of the spirits." Now we point out the primeval as before the creation of heaven and earth, when not a single thought occurs, so when it speaks of emerging from the borders of the primeval and returning to the beginning of the primeval, what is the principle? Nowadays it's really hard to find people who have ever reached the point where not a single thought occurs—how can there be any who have returned to the origin of the primeval?

When it is said that spirit people keep this state, it is just a term; they don't get the principle. In our school, the greathearted give up mundane objects and stop myriad concerns, and still find it hard to attain this path even after ten or twenty years. How much the more so for those who are physically bound up in mundane toil and mentally deficient in mediation and concentration, trying to force themselves to keep this teaching! Indeed, since Shinto has such a profound attainment, isn't it pitiful to think lightly of Buddhism?

Generally speaking, the term *spirit* refers to mind. When mental pollution is eliminated, it's like a mirror being clear—this is called spirit. Therefore the Spirit Vehicle uses a mirror to symbolize its substance. The mind-mirror is originally clear and clean, stable and calm—this is called Kunitokotachi no Mikoto.[36] The mind-mirror is originally round and bright, reflecting everything without exception—this is called Amaterasu Omikami.[37] *The*

---

35. That is, Buddhism.
36. The creator of earth.
37. The sun goddess.

Original Record of the Seat of the Great Spirit Toyoukeko says, "Exercising immense compassion, with independent spiritual power manifesting various forms according to various mentalities, creating expedient ways of welfare, it is represented by the names Soul of the Sun, and Spirit That Illumines the Sky. This is the original substance of all things, liberating all classes."

So it should be realized that the Spirit Vehicle and Buddhism have the same noumenal substance, but neither are beyond the one single truth of seeing nature. If you can understand your own nature, then you merge with the primeval noumenon at the outset; if you then search out the deep meaning within nature, you gradually emerge from its borders and return to the origin of the primordial. Ah, the word *origin* is excruciatingly hard to approach—students of the Spirit Vehicle should not gloss over it!

Also, in the doctrines of Confucius and Mencius, name and reality are used together for the general welfare of the world. Humanity, justice, loyalty, and reciprocity are produced by a single nature. The doctrines of Lao-tzu and Chuang-tzu refute names to get to realities, solely studying the Way and its virtues. Emptiness, nothingness, and spontaneity are produced by a single nature. Therefore Confucius and Mencius never made humanity, justice, and reciprocity out to be the Way, and Lao-tzu and Chuang-tzu never made emptiness, nothingness, and spontaneity out to be the Way. They just imposed names to open up essential roads; these are not what they consider ultimate ends.

Therefore Confucius said, "Do you think I know a lot by broad study? My way is pervaded by unity." Lao-tzu said, "Always desireless to observe the subtle, always desiring to observe the cyclic." Confucius and Mencius disciplined by education; Lao-tzu and Chuang-tzu educated by discipline. Buddha could educate and could discipline. Confucius and Mencius are enriched by Lao-tzu and Chuang-tzu, Lao-tzu and Chuang-tzu are completed by Confucius and Mencius; both doctrines are penetrated by Buddhism, while Buddhism uses the two doctrines to assist. The influence of Confucius and Mencius broadens, the influence of Lao-tzu and Chuang-tzu deepens; the influence of Buddha perfects and clarifies. The teachings of Confucianism and Taoism communicate their wisdom to one era and only benefit human beings, not other forms of life. The knowledge and compassion of the Buddhas is infinitely vast, benefiting beings in all forms of life and comprehending all things in all times.

Nevertheless, even though there are differences in breadth and narrowness, partiality and completeness, the essential import is but one. Some compare Confucius and Lao-tzu to the two lesser vehicles, but without thorough discussion. Now let me discuss this in terms of their teachings. To compare these to the lesser vehicles is all right in respect to having the flaw of bias, but even so this is a question of comparative crudity or precision of verbal instruction; it doesn't mean their ways have that problem.When Confucius and Mencius explained the accumulation of suffering and set up guidelines close to the standards of conduct of the lesser vehicles, they were temporarily teaching the Way in conformity with society; if you don't recognize skill in expedient means, you'll stop halfway. When Lao-tzu and Chuang-tzu repudiated everything based on the way to extinction resembling nirvana with remainder, they were temporarily treating symptoms according to potential; if you don't study the principle of completeness, you'll surely stay in the magic citadel.[38]

It is like Buddha setting up three vehicles; though there is deep meaning, people of small potential all stop at the tracks of the teaching. So it's not the fault of the Way, but the shortcomings of people's faculties and potentials. Zen Master Dazhu Huihai said, "When people of great measure apply them, they're the same; when people of little potential hold to them, they're different." All produce their functions from one nature, but differences in potentials and perceptions make them into three. Confusion and enlightenment come from the person; they are not in the difference or sameness of doctrine.

To generalize about the paths of Shinto, Confucianism, and

38. "The magic citadel" is a pejorative metaphor for nirvana.

Taoism, bodhisattvas teach in response to the times—there has never been a fixed doctrine. Since ancient times the perfectly good have illustrated the Way to their generation, so it was possible to get the essence without use of precepts or formalities. This is why they were of benefit in ancient times. The inferior potentials of later ages are so bound up that they're hard to free, so first they give up social involvements to enter into the path with their whole bodies.

It is like the case of someone traveling a steep road. If he has a lot of baggage, as he runs out of strength he gets so weary he can't get past that stretch of the road. If he has no heavy burden, alone and free, really resolved, he passes directly through the hard incline and is able to reach the end. So cultivating the path in lay life is like traveling far with a heavy load; it takes a long time and hard work, and it is difficult to gain independence. If you give up the world to enter the Dharma, it's like crossing the mountains without baggage; because you're traveling light, it's easy to take the high road.

Now in the method of seeing nature of which I speak, there's no issue of monastic or lay—it's just a matter of setting out as best you can. When the time comes, you'll shed the burden. If you say there are no hindrances in lay life, this is preferring to carry a burden, increasing bondage all the more, tired and suffering forever. Yet those who don't even set out because they're afraid they have a heavy load at present are even further away from home.

Passing a whole lifetime for naught is like water sinking down, eventually to disappear. If people don't cultivate it, their will for enlightenment will eventually die out. If you're like this today, you'll be like this lifetime after lifetime. It would be better to set out as best you can to get onto the right road; then someday the time will come when you shed your burden. Then you can act unconventionally or go with the flow, unimpeded, independent. This is why Buddhism has discipline, concentration, insight, and relinquishment, transcending worldly involvements.

Another problem with lay life is that even if you pass the steep road, even though you enter into knowledge of essential nature, the principles of differentiation will be hard to understand completely.[39] It's like a merchant who has capital but can hardly make a profit because his business strategy is inexpert. Craving and love, emotions and desires, inwardly waste away character, while illusions of name and gain outwardly corrupt behavior. When you are physically and mentally belabored by such things, not only is your strategy with nature inexpert, your consumption is excessive. The thieves are inside, draining your assets, so you cannot succeed in developing rich character.

In this sense, students should not lose their time, whether they're laypeople or monastics. If you're in lay life today, it can't be helped; so you should free yourself as soon as you get the opportunity. On this account there may be those who say there will be no one in the world if all become monastics. This is the theory of earthworms begrudging soil. Now there's no one in the world who doesn't seek wealth and status, but if everyone were wealthy aristocrats, who would be their employees? Who would be the ordinary citizens? But the rich everywhere are decreasing daily, while there are more and more poor. What is that all about?

Everywhere doctors are formulating potent medicines to cure others' illnesses, but there is no end of patients. Hunters chase birds and beasts every day, but they don't diminish. Why would this be considered strange only in Buddhism? The Buddhas and bodhisattvas made universal vows to liberate all beings and never regress, yet the realms of living beings have not ended, because they are infinite.

39. Japanese society was at this time controlled by a caste system constructed to limit the scope of individual and collective experience, knowledge, and initiative. Torei's advocacy of monasticism may be understood in this context of social rigor and stagnation under military rule and hereditary caste, as well as admittedly widespread monastic decadence and official and popular mistrust of monks. It may also be connected, perhaps unconsciously, to his own sickliness. The tendency to promote monasticism as a form of elitism increased as a defensive measure with the restoration of state Shinto and official antagonism to Buddhism in the Meiji era, already foreshadowed in Torei's work a century earlier.

For these reasons, Shinto, Confucianism, and Taoism can only be fulfilled to the maximum extent if you first manage to see nature. If you study all the Buddhist teachings, that can be called being fully equipped. Even attainment of expertise in all the arts of the world is based on the ocean of fundamental nature.

If you're lost and don't know it, you wear out your body pursuing shadows. Therefore if all learners just turn to their own nature and clarify it, investigate it, then the essentials of all the schools will spontaneously become evident. If you seek them outside, that's like the impoverished son who left his father and ran away, seeking food and clothing at random.[40] Can we not feel sorry?

It's like a sickness that has persisted for many years so the mind and energy are exhausted in the extreme, and the spleen and kidneys are drained and depleted. Even acupuncture, moxibustion, and medicine will hardly have any effect. The human body originally has no disease; when there is an empty place inside, then external abnormalities invade it, and that creates the root of disease.

Medicine quells abnormal energies, not mental energy; when abnormal energies are eliminated, mental energy is inherently robust. Even so, when mental energy is exhausted in the extreme, abnormal energies increase, so that the strength of medicine can hardly match it, and therefore the disease cannot be cured. If you yourself nurture your spirit within your body, then your mental energy will gradually fill and won't be affected by abnormalities from outside. Therefore you will also find medicine effective.[41]

It is like the rise or fall of a nation depending on the leadership. If the leadership is right, outsiders dare not invade. So it is with Buddhism; first turn to your own mind and look deeply

40. This is a simile from the *Lotus-sutra*, very commonly used in Zen writings, criticizing the followers of the lesser vehicles for not realizing their own intrinsic buddha-nature.

41. Zen Master Dahui used to prescribe saving mental energy as a Zen exercise, and this is also a key to Taoist healing.

into its original nature, and then conditioned consciousness disappears and enlightened insight appears. All the teachings are understood, without exception.

For this reason, it is not only our school that is based on seeing nature; the other schools in essence all must be based on seeing nature. If you want to study the ideas of a school without seeing nature, even if you study all the Buddhist doctrines, your conditioned consciousness will be as deep-seated as ever, so enlightened insight cannot appear.

When the spirit is not nourished, the torment of sickness increases. When buddha-nature is not revealed, conditioned consciousness increases. The strength of medicine does not overcome the strength of disease; the power of the path does not overcome the power of conditioning. Please use the principles of curing disease to examine thoroughly and contemplate objectively; the paths of difficult practice and easy practice culminate here!

The only exceptions are the inconceivably liberated bodhisattvas who come riding great vows of compassion and temporarily teach lesser doctrines. They sometimes show miraculous powers to open people's minds, taking in those of lowest potential, startling those lacking faith into wakefulness, to create conditions that will produce liberation. This too is one approach to Buddhism, an example of great compassion that is to be valued.

Our school only discusses genuine realization for ordinary people; we do not discuss the domain of secular power. We only choose leaders of Buddhism; we don't ask about other things. If ordinary people don't actually experience it, the true Dharma will die out. If the leaders are intelligent and enlightened, since everything comes from oneself, they directly uphold the doctrine of progressive transcendence to deal with people of the highest potential. For those in middling and lesser categories who hear and believe it, it becomes the finest seed, so they will surely attain the Way in this lifetime or the next life. For those who hear but don't believe it, it will still become a seed of faith, which someday will become deep faith.

Since no one is left out and those of higher, middling, and lesser faculties all attain true genuine Buddhism, what doctrine could add to that? Compared to educating the whole world in hopes of success, educating one ruler is wise, since then everyone in the land will resort to the true teaching. Compared to permanently working for a ruler, discoursing on that path, it is better to inherit the throne yourself and rule the land. When wherever you live is your capital city, wherever you reside is your palace, and your treasury is also as you will, this is called the work of the great person.

As for those in various quarters who are partial to particular scriptures or treatises, or seek the Pure Land arbitrarily, without finding out the fundamental, they become middling and lesser types, so they believe middling and lesser doctrines life after life, generation after generation, attaining middling and lesser paths. Even if they're born in buddha lands, they can't believe the supreme teaching and can't attain the fundamental path.

It is like if you use a fruit for seed, it produces sprouts according to type. For this reason it is said that those who are intense about precepts but lax about the vehicle are alike in the Buddha's congregation even if they become listeners or individual illuminates, but in the realm of buddhahood they are as if deaf and mute. Those who are intense about the vehicle but lax about precepts, seeing and hearing, believing and accepting, will all realize the Way, even if they are of different kinds.

Also, for bodhisattvas of the three vehicles, attainment of buddhahood is remote, after three incalculable aeons, because they neglect the root and pursue the branches, not clarifying their own nature. Bodhisattvas of the One Vehicle realize true awakening at the time of their initial inspiration, because they see nature clearly and can comprehend reality.

Also, the keys of all the schools depend on dominant conditions of accumulated virtue, whereas in the context of seeing nature it's all a matter of a single moment of faith. It's like when you want to go to another province you first need a lot of money, and if you want to enter another's home you first need to establish a good relationship. But to go to your own province you don't need a lot of money, and to return to your own home you don't need a relationship. Everyone, without exception, is endowed with the fundamental great wisdom and great virtue of the buddha-nature—isn't that the best of connections?

ON PRACTICE

The work of right mindfulness is the unsurpassed practice. If you have the work of right mindfulness, you don't get stuck on formal practices and are not concerned with dignified manners. In principle and in fact, sitting and walking, right and wrong, action and repose, truth and untruth, in the world and beyond the world, all that's necessary is not losing right mindfulness.

Now tell me, what precisely is the principle of right mindfulness? Practicing meditation and cultivating concentration is the gist of the work, seeing nature and witnessing the Way is the gist of the work, the interlocking of differentiation is the gist of the work, the one road of progressive transcendence is the gist of the work. The Buddhas of all times only realize the gist of the work of right mindfulness; the masters throughout history have only transmitted the gist of the work of right mindfulness. The five periods and eight doctrines only expound the gist of the work of right mindfulness. The old examples of koans only discuss the gist of the work of right mindfulness.

There is coarse and there is fine, there is shallow and there is deep, there is far and there is near, there is raw and there is ripe. Beginners must make sure; the experienced need to be thorough and precise.

So it is that our school only esteems the work of right mindfulness and does not esteem models of conduct or forms of practice. Why? When right mindfulness is continuous, there is nothing else on your mind; when right mindfulness is continuous, it doesn't differ wherever you are. You completely forget objects before you. This is what Yongjia meant by "seeing the mountains, you forget the Way; seeing the Way, you forget the mountains."

Many of the empty-headed "Zennists" of the last age vaunt their own views; instead of basing it on whether or not the work of right mindfulness is continuous, just because they consider manners and forms to be minor practices, they mistakenly regard license and abandon to be living liberation, freedom, and ease. They all say, "Manners and forms are lesser-vehicle practice; in the school of patch-robe monks, why be bound to forms of practice?" With this, they do their best to provide themselves with objects of enjoyment, form cliques, and seek associates. Unrestrained in their license and abandon, they discard the dignities of monks and blend in with secular styles; disdaining religious talks, they prefer miscellaneous conversation. Losing the work mentally, they strive for amusement. Inside, they lounge around; abroad, they act mad. In extreme cases they frequent the doors of song and dance, go to the brothels and bars; behaving eccentrically, they consider this the transcendental Way of Zen. How miserable! How miserable!

Even if you don't offend, how can the actions you see and hear of be inconsequential? Inwardly compelled by craving, perverted views manifest outwardly, ruining the spiritual body, losing the sense of the Way, and instead spoiling novices, getting them to continue these decadent ways as well. Therefore the dignity of Buddhism is all gone, and the shining example of monkhood has disappeared. Faithful patrons withdraw because of this, while people with perverted ideas increase because of this. They slander the true teaching and demean those of lofty character. Jade is crushed along with rock; gold is scrapped with base metal.

I have heard that in ancient times there was a devil king who promised the Buddha, "Some day I will enter your house, wear your clothes, eat your food, study your path, and expound your doctrine in order to destroy your teaching." Those words have already been proved.

Living liberation is not such a principle. An ancient said, "Kill off the living person, and only then will you see the living person; if you want to attain life, you must seek it in death." This means that when right mindfulness is continuous, you still don't consider it enough when the nature of reality becomes

apparent. When right mindfulness is continuous and you cultivate the path to complete maturity, you still don't consider that
enough. When right mindfulness is continuous and you go beyond the Buddhas and Patriarchs, when you get here, you are free
to act unconventionally or conventionally as expedient, giving
and taking independently. When you let go, even rubble radiates
light; when you hold still, the whole universe loses color.

When you get here, what coarse and fine or deep and shallow
can you talk about? When you get here, what raw and ripe or
near and far can you discuss? Even Buddha Dharma isn't there;
how can there be a mundane world? Even body and mind are
forgotten—where do you see manners and formalities?

When study reaches this, it is called the realm of living liberation, untrammeled and free, clear and unencumbered. Therefore
the reasons students don't get caught up in concern with manners and forms is so they won't lose the work of right mindfulness. The reason fully developed people have no manners or
formalities is that when right mindfulness is present, one forgets
manners and formalities.

If your right mindfulness is present, and continues moment
to moment, in movement you forget movement, in stillness you
forget stillness. In the midst of objects you forget objects; in your
mind you forget mind. Undivided by movement and stillness,
undivided by good and bad, undivided by pain and pleasure, undivided by affliction and enlightenment, undivided by heaven
and hell, those who arrive at this undivided state no longer mind
anything and no longer seek anything. Since they don't seek anything, what indulgence can there be?

Now it's one thing to relinquish manners and formalities, but
what about only indulging in license? Scripture says, "Even the
Dharma is to be relinquished; how much more its contrary."
Once you're undivided, you shouldn't indulge in anything; if you
do, that's not being undivided. If you're not yet undivided, you
should repent—what leisure do you have to indulge your feelings and let your mind go, idly enjoying amusement?

Those who are capable of being undivided no longer seek anything for themselves; their only quest is to liberate the living. They do not indulge themselves; their only indulgence is to liberate the living. They do not act for themselves; they only act to liberate the living. They have no thought for themselves; their only thought is to liberate the living.

Why? Because they themselves have attained an undivided state, whereas all people have not arrived at this realm; with great compassion they magically produce expedients for everyone. All their practices, all their discourses, are for the multitude of the living, not themselves. Indeed, if you want to become undivided out of craving to be seen and heard, this is impossible.

Therefore the wise just stick to maintaining the practice of the work of right mindfulness. Don't stick to any fixations at all. Don't lose right mindfulness wherever you are, and the experience of liberation will naturally come about. When it does, and you see without missing anything, you cannot find anywhere to fixate.

When you get here, then what good state is there to stir your mind and belabor your body, put forth your hands and move your feet, such as could pacify your religious sense? Wrong, wrong! Right where everyone stands there is this unsurpassed practice; let genuine students of the mystery try to discern.

REFERENCES

SCRIPTURES

Buddhist Yoga. Translated by Thomas Cleary. Boston: Shambhala Publications, 1995.

Dhammapada: The Sayings of Buddha. Translated by Thomas Cleary. New York: Bantam Books, 1995.

The Flower Ornament Scripture. Translated by Thomas Cleary. Boston: Shambhala Publications, 1993.

The Sutra of Hui-neng: Grand Master of Zen. Translated by Thomas Cleary. Boston: Shambhala Publications, 1998.

Zen and the Art of Insight. Translated by Thomas Cleary. Boston: Shambhala Publications, 1999.

KOAN COLLECTIONS

The Blue Cliff Record. Translated by Thomas and J. C. Cleary. Boston: Shambhala Publications, 1977.

Book of Serenity. Translated by Thomas Cleary. Boston: Shambhala Publications, 2005.

Secrets of the Blue Cliff Record. Translated by Thomas Cleary. Boston: Shambhala Publications, 2000.

Transmission of Light. Translated by Thomas Cleary. Boston: Shambhala Publications, 2002.

Unlocking the Zen Koan. Translated by Thomas Cleary. Berkeley: North Atlantic Books, 1997.

WRITINGS AND SAYINGS OF ZEN MASTERS

Dream Conversations: On Buddhism and Zen. Translated by Thomas Cleary. Boston: Shambhala Publications, 1994.

The Five Houses of Zen. Translated by Thomas Cleary. Boston: Shambhala Publications, 1997.

Instant Zen: Waking Up in the Present. Translated by Thomas Cleary. Berkeley, North Atlantic Books, 1994.

Kensho: The Heart of Zen. Translated by Thomas Cleary. Boston: Shambhala Publications, 1997.

The Original Face. Translated by Thomas Cleary. New York: Grove Press, 1978.

The Pocket Zen Reader. Translated by Thomas Cleary. Boston: Shambhala Publications, 1999.

Record of Things Heard. Translated by Thomas Cleary. Boulder, Colo.: Prajna Press, 1980.

Swampland Flowers: The Letters and Lectures of Zen Master Ta Hui. Translated by J. C. Cleary. Boston: Shambhala Publications, 2006.

Teachings of Zen. Translated by Thomas Cleary. Boston: Shambhala Publications, 1998.

Timeless Spring. Translated by Thomas Cleary. Tokyo: Weatherhill, 1980.

Zen Antics. Translated by Thomas Cleary. Boston: Shambhala Publications, 1993.

Zen Dawn. Translated by J. C. Cleary. Boston: Shambhala Publications, 2001.

Zen Essence. Translated by Thomas Cleary. Boston: Shambhala Publications, 1988.

Zen Lessons. Translated by Thomas Cleary. Boston: Shambhala Publications, 1989.

Zen Letters. Translated by J. C. and Thomas Cleary. Boston: Shambhala Publications, 2001.

ESOTERIC BUDDHISM

The Ecstasy of Enlightenment. Translated by Thomas Cleary. Boston: Shambhala Publications, 1998.

Twilight Goddess. By Thomas Cleary and Sartaz Aziz. Boston: Shambhala Publications, 2000.

TENDAI BUDDHISM

The Buddhist I Ching. Translated by Thomas Cleary. Boston: Shambhala Publications, 1987.

Stopping and Seeing. Translated by Thomas Cleary. Boston: Shambhala Publications, 1997.

KEGON BUDDHISM

Entry into the Inconceivable. By Thomas Cleary. Honolulu: University of Hawaii, 1983.

Entry into the Realm of Reality. By Thomas Cleary. Boston: Shambhala Publications, 1989.

ZEN AND JAPANESE CULTURE

The Japanese Art of War. By Thomas Cleary. Boston: Shambhala Publications, 1991.

Samurai Wisdom. By Thomas Cleary. North Clarendon, Vt.: Tuttle Publishing, 2009.

The Soul of the Samurai. By Thomas Cleary. North Clarendon, Vt.: Tuttle Publishing, 2004.

Training the Samurai Mind. By Thomas Cleary. Boston: Shambhala Publications, 2008.

Printed in the United States
By Bookmasters